# Renewing Hope

## Is There Room For Hope In A World Like This?

Daniel Simundson

Fairway Press, Lima, Ohio

RENEWING HOPE

FIRST EDITION
Copyright @ 2001 by
Daniel Simundson

All rights reserved. No portion of this book may be reproduced or utilized in any form or by any means, electronic or mechanical including photocopying, without permission in writing from the publisher. Inquiries should be addressed to: Fairway Press, 517 South Main Street, P.O. Box 4503, Lima, Ohio 45802-4503.

Library Of Congress Control Number: 2001 131707

SBN 0-7880-1691-1               PRINTED IN U.S.A

*To Sally*
*Who lived and died in hope*

# Is There Room For Hope In A World Like This?

# Preface

This book is a series of 52 reflections on the biblical theme of hope. The intent is to examine carefully the human need for hope from several different angles, with the Bible constantly in conversation with our human experience. For 29 years I have been a teacher of the Old Testament. Prior to my graduate work in Bible, I was a parish pastor and a hospital chaplain. In this volume, I have attempted to draw on all that experience, trying to cross barriers bertween a scholarly and a devotional study of the Bible. I write as one who is a biblical scholar and knows the Bible from that perspective. I am also concerned for the way people of faith read the Bible, looking for a word of God, trying to find answers to their deepest questions, reaching out for comfort and assurance about their future.

The book could be used in a number of different ways. It is not written in scholarly language so it should be accessible to laypeople and clergy alike. One could read it as a devotional book—one section at a time, perhaps for morning or evening prayer. A group of people could use it as a Bible study resource, reading one or more chapters each session. There is at least one Bible reference for each section so they could engage directly with the Bible as well as with my words. A pastor might find some inspiration here for a series of sermons (perhaps a Lenten series). And, I hope, the material is written with enough seriousness, that it might be of some value for a college or seminary course that is working on the subject of hope, especially as presented in the Bible. I have gathered the shorter pieces into seven larger categories that have their own coherence, and the whole book has a logical movement from beginning to end.

Hope is something we all want and need and which, when it comes, is a gift from God. My personal hope is that this small volume may be of some assistance to others as they walk in hope throughout their earthly journey.

Daniel J. Simundson

# Outline

### A. What is hope?
1. To have a good future (Prov. 23:18)
2. To hope <u>for</u> and to hope <u>in</u> (Ps. 130:7)
3. Hope and faith are closely related (Heb. 11:1)
4. Human relationships can sustain hope (Ps. 133:1,3)
5. Hope is not the same as optimism (Matt. 24:35)
6. Hope is elusive (John 3:8)
7. Often, hope is simply a matter of patience (Ps. 13:1; James 5:7a, 8b)

### B. God's response to our need for hope
1. Clothes for Adam and Eve (Gen. 3:15, 21)
2. God promises, "Never again." (Gen. 9:11)
3. Many obstacles in the way of the promise (Heb. 11:8-12)
4. Hunger in the wilderness (Exod. 16:1-3)
5. David's sins are forgiven (2 Sam. 12:13-14)
6. Habakkuk waits for the Lord (Hab. 1:13; 2:1-4)
7. Let Job say how bad it is (Job 7:6; 13:15a)
8. Dreams of peace for this world and beyond (Isa. 11:1-9)
9. A reality check for Jeremiah (Jer. 12:1-5)
10. The long wait is almost over (Rom. 8:18-25)

### C. Hope for what? (The content of hope)
1. Food, water, and a place to live (Ps. 145:15-16)
2. Protection from danger (Ps. 27:11)
3. That good will remain and the bad will go away (Eccles. 12:1-8; Job 1:5)
4. Friends, counselors, human support (Philip. 2:1-2)
5. God's presence as forgiver, not condemner (Ps. 139:1-12)
6. Justice, a moral world (Job 9:24)
7. To be remembered well (Job 19:23-27)
8. If what we hoped for does not come (2 Cor 12:7-10)

### D. Hope in whom (or in what)?
1. Not in things of this world (1 Cor. 15:19)
2. Not in power or might (Ps. 33:16-17)
3. Not in the "system" (John 16:33; 18:36a)
4. Not in our health (Mark 5:34)
5. Not in wisdom (Job 28:28)
6. Not in peace of mind or psychological well-being (John 14:27)
7. Not in a God we can manipulate or control (Matt. 7:7-8a)
8. Only in the God of the Bible (Exod. 20:2-3)

### E. The transition from despair to hope
1. Hope when there is no hope (Jer. 20:18)
2. From lament to praise (Ps. 13:1a, 5-6)
3. Hope when the outcome is in doubt (Lam. 3:19-33)
4. Job's spiritual journey (Job 42:1-6)
5. Suffering produces hope (Rom. 5:1-5)

### F. Hope beyond the present world
1. Community in life and death (Gen. 49:29-50:3)
2. Job almost believes (Job 14:7-19)
3. Dry bones will live again (Ezek. 37:1-14)
4. The Lord will swallow up death forever (Isa. 25:6-9; 26:16-19)
5. Resurrection followed by judgment (Dan. 12:1-2)
6. Promise and warning from Jesus (Luke 16:19-31)
7. Today with me in Paradise (Luke 23:39-43)
8. Jesus speaks about eternal life in John's Gospel (John 3:16; 11:1-44; 14:1-3)
9. Paul's indifference toward death (Philip. 1:12-26)
10. What is a "spiritual body?" (1 Cor. 15)

### G. Speaking of hope to others
1. Listen before speaking (Job 2:11-13)
2. Don't promise too much (Prov. 25:20a)
3. When to speak explicitly about hope? (Rom. 10:14)
4. Dare to show your love and concern (1 John 4:10-12)

## A. What is Hope?

We all need hope. Without it, the future seems frightening, dominated by unknowns that are beyond our control. We would like to understand hope with our minds, but mostly we want to experience it. We want to hang on to the hope that we have and regain the hope that has been lost. In this series of reflections we will walk together through the Bible to remind ourselves of how God speaks to our need for hope. We begin wih several statements about hope that will help us map out our journey. We will keep them in mind as we follow the theme of hope through the Bible.

### 1. To Have a Good Future

"Surely there is a future, and your hope will not be cut off" (Prov. 23:18). To live in hope is to expect, with confidence, that we will have a good future. That is about as good a short, simple, direct definition of hope as any.

Sometimes people have come to the dreary conclusion that they have no future. A teenager is overwhelmed by the dangers that confront her personal world. There is violence in the school and on the neighborhood streets. New diseases appear, like AIDS, out of nowhere, with no cure in sight and thousands of lives at risk. Will intimacy ever be possible in such a fearful world? And the whole planet could dissolve in a nuclear holocaust even before one has time to become an adult. How can we plan for the future when we wonder if we will ever reach adulthood?

The woman who has just received a diagnosis of cancer wonders if she has a future. The word "cancer" has struck terror in her soul. She can see pain and suffering in her immediate future and then the awesome threat of nothingness, obliteration, death. While waiting for all the tests to be completed, the tension becomes almost unbearable. Is this going to be the end? When she talks with her husband and children, what will they say to each other about the plans they have made for next summer, for the daughter's wedding, or how they will spend their retirement? Is everything on hold? Do they proceed as if nothing has changed? Is there a future for her, with her family and loved ones and familiar surroundings?

Since we all must die, we are faced with questions about what comes after our death. Is this all there is? At the time of death, can we still say that we have a future? And, if we do, will it be good?

In order to live in hope, we must know that we have a future, that we are not speeding down a dead end street that has no exit. But hope is more than mere quantity, more time, more years, even on into eternity. Not just any old future will do. If our expectation for what lies ahead is to be hope and not fear, apprehension, despair, even terror, we need the assurance that our future will be good.

So what would it take to make our future good so that we can live in hope? These are some thoughts that come to my mind if my future is to be good. Perhaps your list would be similar. I want as much love and life and laughter as I can get and as little suffering as possible. I need the confidence that my loved ones (and myself) will be protected from danger, that pain will not be too severe for us to bear, that evil will not have the last word. I want my relationships of love and intimacy to continue so that I will never be left completely alone. I need to be assured (at some times more than at others) that God will never abandon me, that the Power behind all that there is will be on my side and not against me. Since life is so short, grief is so painful, and fear of our own death so strong, we all need assurance that there is more to human existence than we can see from this side of the grave. And, both in this life and the next, we need the confidence that God is always more concerned to forgive than to punish.

To live in hope is to know that we have a future, that our existence has a continuity that cannot be cut off even by the most threatening dangers, and that our future will be good. God once spoke these words of hope through Jeremiah, "For surely I know the plans I have for you, plans for your welfare and not for harm, to give you a future with hope" (Jer. 29:11).

### 2. To hope _for_ and to hope _in_ (Ps. 130:7)

There are particular things _for_ which I hope. My hope has a specific content. I can give you a list if you ask me, "What do you hope for in life?" For example, most of us hope _for_ good health, a happy marriage, meaningful work, avoidance of suffering, a long life, good friends, economic security, and so on. Sometimes, what we hope for is more trivial: a nice day for the picnic, a win for the Twins, a parking place close to the theater, a good day at work.

Or, when we speak of hope, we may refer to the persons, ideas, or systems in which we place our hopes. We often put our future in the hands of certain authorities in whom we hope: parents, pastors, teachers, scientists, medical experts, government leaders, God. As long as we believe that persons whom we have trusted are on our side, looking out for our behalf, with the wisdom and power to make our future a good and safe place, then we can continue to be hopeful.

Sometimes, we put our hope for the future not so much in individuals but in structures or systems which society has set up and promoted as ways of maintaining the general welfare of the people. And so we are expected to place our hopes (our trust, if you will) in the free enterprise system, the whole judicial process (including the police, the courts, and the legal profession), the military-industrial establishment, the health care system, and the government's responsibility to provide welfare for the needy and social security for us all. If these systems work as they are supposed to, in a way that is fair and just, we can remain confident about both our own personal future and the future of our society as a whole.

Generally, it is much easier for one to continue in an attitude of hope if one has not been disappointed by failure to receive what one has hoped for or has not lost confidence in the person or thing in which one had hoped. Many become depressd and in despair of the future because they have invested so much of themselves in the content of their hope. They hoped for a life of health and well being but have been forced to spend years coping with a chronic illness. They hoped for an ideal family like those they learned about in Sunday School and on the television, but their marriage was always rocky and now their children are having a hard time building lasting relationships. Meaningful work, economic security, and other youthful visions of the future never quite lived up to expectations. Hope was tied to very specific aspirations, and with the loss of those dreams, hope has gone also.

Further, in our day, many have been abused and hurt and disappointed by those in authority, those in whom they had placed their hope. They find it difficult to trust anymore, and, without trust, hope is very hard to maintain. If you cannot depend on those whose responsibility is to lead us into a good future—parents, teachers, pastors, political leaders—then is it possible to trust anyone? And often, it is not only individuals who fail us. It is the system, society in general. How are persons to maintain hope if experience has taught them to be very skeptical about the police, courts, lawyers, legislators, businessmen, pastors, doctors and drug companies and hospital administrators?

We hope for and we hope in. Whether or not we are able to hope is often conditioned by how we respond to our failures to achieve what we hoped for or our disillusionment with those in whom we had entrusted our hope. For a believer, true hope is able to rise above these disappintments and to continue in spite of life's darker experiences. It is hope in God that makes this possible. "O Israel, hope in the Lord! For with the Lord there is steadfast love, and with him is great power to redeem" (Ps. 130:7).

### 3. Hope and faith are closely related (Heb. 11:1)

Both faith and hope are relatively easy when everything is going well, life is good, everyone is healthy, and we are surrounded by people who love us. When our lives take a sudden downturn, both faith and hope become more difficult.

Frank Smith had been a Christian all his life. His faith in God was sincere and strong. His daily prayers always included a special word of thanks for his wonderful family and a request that God would continue to keep safe those who were most dear to him. The future for him and his family looked good. And then came the terrible day when the policeman stood at the door and told him about the accident. He was never the same again after that. The son in whom he had invested so much love and hope was dead, killed in an automobile crash a few weeks before graduating from medical school.

He entered a severe crisis of faith. Questions about God flooded his mind. He could not turn them off. Was this God's doing? Why did God let it happen? Can there possibly be any meaning to this? Does God enter into our lives in a personal way to guard us from danger? Or are we completely at the mercy of chance, arbitrary events that simply happen, as we drift aimlessly through a life that is filled with hazards? If God did not act to prevent this most terrible of personal tragedies, how can we trust God to do so in the future? How can we continue in hope if we have lost confidence that God walks with us to make our future good? This father mourns his loss of hope and faith along with the loss of his son. He knows he cannot get his son back. But will he ever be able to believe in the goodness and power of God again? Will hope ever return?

Faith and hope go together. In times of spiritual emptiness, both faith and hope need to be renewed. Whatever strengthens faith will also restore hope, and vice versa. But both faith and hope are elusive, hard to define and difficult to create either in oneself or in others. Often, we are frustrated and impatient as we wait for God to come to renew in us the faith and hope that we cannot bring to reality all by ourselves.

In Heb. 11:1, we read, "Now faith is the assurance of things hoped for, the conviction of things not seen." Hope and faith both have to do with an attitude toward the future. Both speak of confidence that God will provide those things for which we long but cannot see because the future is not fully known to us. Faith and hope move together in our relationship with God.

In 1 Cor. 13:13, Paul adds still a third of the great words that describe the life of a Christian person—love. "And now faith, hope, and love abide, these three; and the greatest of these is love." Faith and hope are also intricately related to love—love of God and of neighbor. Paul dares to state the priority of love in this listing of Christian attitudes. This may suggest that in our search for spiritual assurance in the midst of a personal crisis of faith and/or hope, we do best to shift our attention to love. Preoccupation with efforts to instill hope and faith in oneself may be self-defeating. Begin with love and let hope and faith renew themselves quietly as you concentrate more on the other than yourself.

Faith (trust) and hope are inextricably bound together. Faith in a loving, present, wise, and powerful God gives us the confidence to hope even when all our earthly hopes have failed us. "For you, O Lord, are my hope, my trust, O Lord, from my youth" (Ps. 71:5).

### 4. Human relationships can sustain hope (Ps. 133:1, 3)

The first thing she did after the initial shock of the diagnosis was to go to the phone and call someone else who had also endured breast cancer. She needed to express her fears to a person who would understand, not just in a general human way, but in the sharing of an experience. Most of all she wanted to talk to those who had survived for a long time, who could remind her that there is a life after breast cancer, who were living examples of the hope for which she was grasping.

Hope is closely tied to our relationships, on both the divine and human level. The stronger our faith in God, the easier it is to hope. On the human level, too, our ability to hope has been affected by the way important figures (parents, teachers, pastors, doctors, etc.) in our lives have or have not lived up to the expectations we have laid on them. Hope comes easier and is more likely to survive the storms of life, in one who had a secure, nurturing, loving childhood. One who learned to trust at an early age will ordinarily be a more hopeful person. When troubles come, as they do to all regardless of heredity and upbringing, those from loving families will have certain resources available for the sustaining and renewing of hope. They will know that they can return to their family when necessary, that there will be support and love, that they will not be rejected. Further, they will have learned how to build other communities of support. They can be confident that they will not have to face the future alone. Someone will be there with them to share both the good and the bad.

Those who were not blessed with such hope-sustaining relationships early in life may find them later. Hope is not lost because one was born into the wrong family. Perhaps some may need counseling from a qualified, understanding person. Others may need role models of love and acceptance which they had missed in their formative years. The church, one hopes, should be a place where such communities of hope can be formed.

In our day, a myriad of support groups has arisen to provide specialized resources for the renewal of hope. Those who have been through painful, sometimes almost hopeless, experiences meet together to share themselves with others who are struggling with the same kind of suffering. The alcoholic, the parent whose child has just died, the breast cancer survivor, the widow or widower, or the recently unemployed find new hope by sharing their pain and success, their tragedy and their humor, with each other. There is no false optimism, no simplistic solutions, no hesitancy to speak honestly and forthrightly, no hiding from reality. And out of this comes hope—a hope that is built on the strength of human love and community. These groups do not promise more than they can deliver, but they do revive hope for people at a time in their lives when this is desperately needed.

Hospices for the terminally ill are a special case of providing hope, even in the face of imminent death, through the expression of human concern and care. Those who are unfamiliar with such places find it difficult to imagine how they can be communities of hope. The power of human love to renew and sustain hope is remarkable.

There is a lesson here for those times when we would like to say or do something that will inspire hope in someone else. Too often we approach such a task as an intellectual challenge, as if the right word, biblical quotation, or theological argument will convince this person that hope is still a viable option for her. And then we fret and feel inadequate as a comforter because we are not clever enough to make a convincing case for hope in light of her terrible predicament. It may well be that we best convey hope not by what we say, not by making the best case for hope through some brilliant intellectual presentation, but by being a loving person, part of a human community that through its concern for one in trouble is able to renew and sustain hope. "How very good and pleasant it is when kindred live together in unity. It is like the dew of Hermon, which falls on the mountains of Zion. For there the Lord ordained his blessing, life forevermore" (Ps. 133:1, 3).

### 5. Hope is not the same as optimism (Matt. 24:35)

Several years ago on a trip to Israel, ex-President Jimmy Carter was asked if he was optimistic about the possibility of a peace settlement between the state of Israel and the Palestinians. He replied that he was not optimistic, but that he was not without hope. He was clearly making a distinction between his understanding of optimism and hope. Optimism is a positive attitude toward the future, a predisposition always to expect the best, a confidence that everything will work out no matter how bad the situation appears to be. This is similar to hope, but with some important differences.

Optimism seems often to be tied to a particular personality type. Some folks are bouncy and upbeat all the time. It is part of their nature always to look on the bright side. Those who are of a more pessimistic (they would probably call themselves "realists") inclination find it very difficult to put on an optimistic face. It just does not fit. But it is possible for them to be hopeful.

Optimism describes an outlook toward the future that is generally more superficial than hope. It may have some difficulty including the suffering, sin, evil, and tragedies of life into its view of the world. This may lead to denial of reality, the refusal to admit that things are as bad as they are, an inability to identify with the pain of others and to bring them comfort. Though most of us enjoy the company of a dedicated optimist most of the time, we find they are generally not very helpful when we are in deep trouble and need someone to meet us in the depths of our suffering. Further, optimists, themselves, may be vulnerable to a severe disillusionment if their own life experiences take a turn for the worse. If they had put their hopes in things of this world in the naive expectation that good will always win and healing will always come and relationships will never be broken and doubts will never overwhelm, then they may be subject to a great letdown if such unpleasantness enters their lives. And when that happens, what they will need is hope and not a new injection of optimism.

Hope is more profound than optimism. It can survive with or without success in this world. It can stare evil in the face, deal with human sin, even look death in the eye, and remain intact. Our Christian faith does not present a rosy, optimistic picture of what the world is like or the way humans have acted throughout history. From the beginning to the end of the biblical story, we have a sorry account of disobedience, distrust, hostility, war, punishment for sin, threats of dire consequences for continued rebellion against God, and even the prediction of an endtime in which the world as we know it will be completely destroyed. There is not a lot of optimism in that picture. But there is hope. From the first sin in the garden to the end-of-the-world predictions in Revelation, God has been at work, trying to win us back, reaching into our lives with little victories that give us the anticipation of greater victories in the future, never leaving us to be destroyed by our own deeds. The cruel reality of the crucifixion gives way to hope in the glorious message of Easter.

Jesus said, "Heaven and earth will pass away, but my words will not pass away" (Matt. 24:35; also Luke 21:33). Do not put your hopes on things of this earth. The earth, and even the heaven (sky, perhaps, or our images of what heaven might be) will pass away. There is nothing permanent in heaven or earth on which to pin your hopes. That sounds almost like pessimism. At any rate, it is surely not optimism. "But my words will not pass away." There is our source of hope. Even the entire universe may go up in smoke, but Jesus' words of promise, God's concern and love for us, will never go away. This is God's world and we belong to God and God will have the last say. We have a future that nothing can destroy. And God will be there, and it will be good.

### 6. Hope is elusive (John 3:8)

The two men were similar in many ways. They had known each other since childhood and lived all their life in the same town. They attended the same church, had learned the same catechism from the same pastor, and heard the same sermons over all those years. And their wives, also close friends, had died within a few months of each other. But their reactions were very different. Though the pain never completely disappeared, Fred was soon able to smile again, to resume a meaningful life, and to face the future with hope. Not so for William. His faith in God was shattered. He became a semi-recluse. He refused to attend church anymore. His anger at God would not go away. Hope had disappeared from his life. Obviously, he did not like feeling and thinking this way. But he didn't know what to do about it. Two men from very similar backgrounds—one with renewed hope and one without. Why such a difference?

Hope is elusive. It is not easy to define, to achieve, or to recover if lost. It comes and it goes. It is affected, modified, and changed by our experiences, but has an inner quality of its own that is not predictable. It may be weakened but could be strengthened by the ups and downs of life. Some find hope renewed in the midst of tragedy. Others become hopeless when confronted by similar circumstances. Many wish they could be hopeful, but don't know how to achieve that desired state. Others desperately wish they knew what to do to renew hope in their loved ones. Hope is elusive.

Hope is hard to define and analyze. We can think about it and say something about what it is and what it is not, as we have already begun to do. We can compare it to something similar, like optimism. But in the end, we are forced to admit that hope is something of a mystery. Some people have it and some do not. It is an inner quality, related to but not completely determined by one's relationships with God and humanity. Whether or not we are able to hope may even be subject to heredity, the chemical balances in our body, or other forces we do not understand. Hope is elusive.

Hope is hard to achieve. It takes more than intellectual argument, quotes from supportive poetry, or the reading of carefully selected biblical texts to instill hope. And yet all those things might help. It takes more than a loving family or a support group that will allow the freedom to express pain and will stay with one during periods of hopelessness. A person who has such loving encouragement may have a better chance to recover hope than one who is forced to endure suffering alone. But there is no guarantee. There is nothing that we can do that will have absolutely predictable results. Hope is elusive, mysterious, beyond our ability to control and manipulate, either in ourselves or in those for whom we care.

Once lost, hope is hard to recover. It is a bitter truth that we often lose hope at the time when we need it the most. During the good times, one does not bother to think much about hope. It is a silent attitude toward life that does not seem to need analysis because everything is working as it should. But when disaster hits, something unexpected destroys the orderly structure of the way life has been and should continue to be, then one searches and grasps for hope. What had been an easy and natural part of one's life, not requiring much thought or effort, has now become a problem that cannot be solved by one's own efforts.

Hope is elusive—hard to define and analyze, hard to achieve if we don't have it, and hard to recover when lost. In these respects it is much like faith, which is also a mystery. We do what we can to enhance faith and hope in ourselves and others. But when all is said and done, the mystery remains. Some are blessed to believe and some struggle constantly with their faith. And so it is with hope. "The wind blows where it chooses, and you hear the sound of it, but you do not know where it comes from or where it goes. So it is with everyone who is born of the Spirit" (John 3:8). And so we turn ourselves over to God, confident that it is God's Spirit that can inspire faith and hope in us and that God does indeed want that for us.

### 7. Often, hope is simply a matter of patience

"How long, O Lord? Will you forget me forever? How long will you hide your face from me?" (Ps. 13:1).

"Be patient, therefore, beloved, until the coming of the Lord... Strengthen your hearts for the coming of the Lord is near" (James 5:7a, 8b).

It is as if James is talking to the Psalmist. "Hang in there. It won't be much longer till relief comes." An important element in hope is patience. There is nothing glamorous, romantic, magical, or mysterious about this aspect of hope. It is simply a matter of sticking it out, not giving in, until something good finally happens. In some ways, sheer persistence, even stubbornness, is closely akin to hope.

One of the Old Testament Hebrew words for hope can be translated as either "wait" or "hope." The context will determine which is the best translation. Usually, when God is the one for whom a person waits, the meaning moves toward hope. In many places the words "hope," "wait," and "patience" can be used interchangeably. Sometimes these words appear in parallel with each other.

Job is losing hope, and he expresses his despair this way: "What is my strength, that I should wait? And what is my end that I should be patient?" (Job 6:11). He no longer has the strength to wait. Patience has left him. Or, to put it another way, he has no hope.

In the Psalms we read: "I believe that I shall see the goodness of the Lord in the land of the living. Wait for the Lord; be strong, and let your heart take courage; wait for the Lord" (27:13-14). "And now, O Lord, what do I wait for? My hope is in you" (39:7). "I wait for the Lord, my soul waits, and in his word I hope; my soul waits for the Lord more than those who watch for the morning" (130:5-6).

We see this overlapping of hoping and waiting several times in the book of Isaiah: "I will wait for the Lord who is hiding his face from the house of Jacob, and I will hope in him" (8:17).
"But those who wait for the Lord shall renew their strength, they shall mount up with wings like eagles" (40:31a).

In the wonderful eighth chapter of Romans, Paul says, "For in hope we were saved. Now hope that is seen is not hope. For who hopes (some ancient authorities read "waits") for what is seen? But if we hope for what we do not see, we wait for it with patience" (8:24-25).

What is it that turns mere waiting into hope, as in these biblical examples? Surely these are not calls to stoicism, grim proclamations that we should accept our fate and find some way to carry on regardless of the misfortune that has come our way. If that was all there was, these would be expressions of fatalism, not words about hope. In this biblical view "waiting with patience" becomes an equivalent of hope because the focus is on God. By pointing toward God, we are reminded of all that God has done for us in the past and God's promises about our future. When prophets and psalmists and apostles express their willingness to wait they are not being heroic or courageous or stoic. They do not like what is going on around them. They recognize that the present situation is intolerable and will have to change. But there is a way out. We are not locked into the inevitability of the way things are now. God knows what we are enduring and God will act to see that a new day will dawn. We may not know when or where. We may wish that it would come sooner rather than later. But we, like the biblical writers, can have complete confidence that the day of deliverance will come. Sure knowledge of that makes our waiting tolerable and, in fact, turns it into hope.

## B. God's Response to our Need for Hope

The Bible records a consistent story of human need for hope and God's action or words of promise to address the human predicament. From beginning to end, in Old and New Testaments, God responds positively to renew hope in those who, for one reason or another, have lost the ability to hope and are no longer confident that they have a good future. Though, from the human side, we are tempted to give up on hope, God has not given up on us.

### 1. Clothes for Adam and Eve (Gen. 3:15, 21)

What a beautiful world God had made! God took special delight in the creation, pausing after each stage to gaze on it and, with satisfaction, note that "it was good." And the climax, the crowning achievement, was the creation of the human beings. They were the ones with whom God would have a special relationship. Though not gods, the humans were "in the image of God," capable of communing with God in a way not possible for God's other creatures.

But with the special relationship came responsibilities for the care of the creation and the necessity for trust in God's counsel and obedience to God's commands. And there were certain risks because the humans were aware of their limitations. They could not see into the future and be certain what was in store for them. Therefore, they were forced to be dependent on God and to trust that God's warnings were for their own advantage. When God told them that they would die if they ate from one of the trees in the garden, a seed of distrust emerged. Why was God holding something back from them? Were there some secrets that they might discover so they would not be forced to depend on God for everything that they did not know? They were vulnerable to the wily inducements of the snake. Their distrust led to disobedience, disobedience led to guilt, guilt led to fear and the effort to hide from God. Finally, God responded with curses on the snake, the woman, and the man (Gen. 3:14-19). The consequences of sin, defying God's specific orders, are severe.

So now what? The beautiful experiment had gone badly. In fact, it was a disaster. Faith (or trust) in God had changed into distrust and now the first representatives of the human race had to face the terrible results of their sin. What hope could remain after the terrible story of the fall? It seems that God had responded with a curse rather than a word of hope.

But if we read carefully, we can see two statements of hope in the midst of the dreadful curses. Though the penalty for their disobedience seems quite harsh, though the human race will be forced to endure many hardships and much suffering (of which the list of curses is only an example), there is still hope. God has not abandoned the creation. Two promises are given—one for the larger, long-term life of humanity on the planet; the other for the specific immediate problem facing our first parents. God speaks a word of hope for humanity in general; God also knows and addresses the specific need for hope in the lives of individuals. God sees both the big picture and the little needs that we bring to his presence. And God responds accordingly.

First, the Christian church has found in the midst of the curse on the snake the first expression of the Gospel, a promise from God that though the Evil One may win some victories in this life, God will at the right time send one who will defeat evil once and for all. "I will put enmity between you and the woman, and between your offspring and hers; he will strike your head, and you will strike his heel" (Gen. 3:15). God will act to redeem the world, to return it to what God intended from the beginning.

Second, God also pays attention to a minor crisis for Adam and Eve. They are now conscious of their nakedness. Their trust in God and each other has now turned to guilt and fear. They want to hide, to cover themselves, both literally and figuratively, so no one will see them open and exposed. And so God Almighty, the maker of heaven and earth, the transcendant and mysterious God of the universe, becomes a seamstress. God meets these people in their distorted and frightened circumstances and provides what they need. "And the Lord God made garments of skins for the man and for his wife, and clothed them" (Gen. 3:21). What a wonderful picture of concern and care for indivduals who need something, maybe even a relatively small or trivial thing, to revive their hope.

From the beginning of time, God has responded to human need for hope, both in the promises of a Savior who will come to save the world gone awry, but also in the everyday trials of individuals like us.

### 2. God promises, "Never again." (Gen. 9:11)

God has been pushed to the extreme by human sin and is strongly tempted to abandon the world and all of humanity to destruction, to give up the whole enterprise as an experiment that went bad. Who needs the agony of watching these human beings inflict pain and suffering on each other in defiance of what they have been told.? It is as if God has to decide once and for all whether there is a future for the relationship between God and human beings. The whole sorry mess could end before we get to chapter 7 of Genesis. Since we are still here, thinking about these matters, it is clear that God decided that the human race should continue. Further, God promised never to destroy the earth, no matter how much we provoke God and no matter how much pain we bring to God's own heart (Gen. 6:6).

For some reason that mystifies us humans, God wants a relationship with us and cannot bring himself to close off completely that possibility. God's impulse to blot out humankind was quickly modified by the decision to save Noah and his family. This wouldn't be the end of the human race after all. Further, once the flood waters had receded, God resolved never to do it again. "As long as the earth endures, seedtime and harvest, cold and heat, summer and winter, day and night, shall not cease" (Gen. 8:22).

As a sign of the new covenant, God put the rainbow in the sky, a reminder to both humans and God that such horror would never happen again. "I establish my covenant with you that never again shall all flesh be cut off by the waters of a flood and never again shall there be a flood to destroy the earth" (Gen. 9:11). To be sure, modern science has other ways to explain the presence of the rainbow. But those worldly explanations need not detract from this story. The rainbow remains as a symbol for God's promise that

God has pledged to hang in there with us for the long haul. No matter how severely tested God will not destroy what God has created out of love. And so, remembering that promise, every time we see a rainbow, our hope for the future of our world and all of humanity can be renewed.

In a world confronted with many threats to the environment (pollution, wasting of natural resources, over-population) and the danger of nuclear incineration, the promise to Noah remains as a beacon of hope. But one caution remains, lest we become too smug and comfortable, resting too confidently in this hopeful word. We humans have some responsibility if the future of the planet is to be good and not catastrophic. The intention of God not to destroy the world and not to end the relationship with people is clear from the conclusion to the flood story. What is not clear is whether God will prevent us from destroying ourselves.

With Noah and his family we can go forward in hope, knowing that God will not destroy. But, since God, even though pained by human sin, has decided to keep the human experiment going, we continue to live in a world not yet brought to perfection. The positive side of God's decision to stay with the human race has a negative side as well, both for God and for us. God continues to grieve for the hurts of humanity. We continue to endure those hurts. We Christians know of another later effort that God will make to reach out to the fallen world, not to destroy but to redeem, by sending his own son.

### 3. Many obstacles in the way of the promise (Heb. 11:8-12)

Our hope may be assaulted by an accumulation of negative life experiences. Though we are firmly planted in a relationship of trust in God, starting with the conviction that God will see that all comes out for the best, we may begin to waver when obstacles continue to loom in front of us. Each little delay, disappointment, and hurt chips away at our hope. We wonder how much we can take before hope turns to despair and faith turns to doubt.

Consider Abraham, the classic Old Testament example of a person of faith. Since hope and faith are so closely connected, he is also a model of the believer who lives in hope. Heb. 11:8-12 summarizes the life of Abraham, with an emphasis on his faith and hope in the promises of God.

When God told Abraham to pack up and go off to a distant land, he went. Surely, he could not know what his future would hold, what the land would be like, what opposition he would meet there. But God told him to go and he put his future in God's hands. For each of us, every new day is a walk into the unknown. For Abraham and Sarah, like refugees and immigrants of every age, the unknown was monumental. People usually do not take on such huge life-changing moves unless their present situation is so bad that the attraction of a new place, even with all its unknowns, is better than staying where they are. Abraham's trust and hope in God gave him the courage to make the move.

God promised Abraham and Sarah that it would be good for them in the new land. They would be the parents of many people, a multitude of persons as numerous as the stars in the sky or the sand of the sea. That was the promise that sustained them and gave them hope as they set off to the west, away from home and all that was familiar. They had hope because they believed what God had said. But it was not a straight road to the fulfillment of those promises. Abraham became the prime example of the person of faith who remained trusting and hopeful, persistent and patient, even though one obstacle after another seemed to make the promise forever unattainable.

You cannot be the ancestors of a mighty nation if you have no children. It takes at least one to get started, to move ahead even one generation. Abraham and Sarah became impatient at times. Though they are good models for us, they were not without their moments of human weakness. Hagar conceived Ishmael and then both were driven away by Sarah's insistence and Abraham's indifference. Sarah could not suppress her laughter when told that she would bear a child in her old age. Finally, when a son, Isaac, was born, God tested Abraham's faith with the terrible directive to kill his only son, the one for whom he had waited all these years, the visible sign that the promise might one day be complete, the hope for his old age and the next generation. Abraham survived even this test of faith (and so did Isaac, for that matter). No obstacle to the promise, no amount of waiting in frustration for God to act, no detour or roadblock or booby trap was sufficient to destroy the hope and faith of Abraham.

A few lessons to consider from Abraham and Sarah: God's promises can be trusted. Our spiritual pilgrimage may not be completely smooth in spite of our confidence when we begin the journey. Progress toward achievement of our hopes may be considerably slower than we like. Sometimes, complete fulfillment may not come even within our own lifetime (Abraham was only the first step in God's plan to create and save a great people) and we must trust God to continue what has begun with us. No obstacles (even old age in the case of Abraham and Sarah) will be able to block forever the fulfillment of God's promises. God will be with us along the way, as we journey into the unknown, and will work in and with us to keep our hopes alive when we begin to waver.

### 4. Hunger in the wilderness (Exod. 16:1-3)

The Hebrew slaves in Egypt suffered terribly under their taskmasters. They dreamed of freedom, release from the heavy and difficult work from which they received no just reward. They cried out to God in despair, hardly daring to hope. And God heard, sent them Moses, and through a series of terrible miracles convinced the Egyptians that it would be better to send the Hebrews away than to risk further plagues.

So now they were wandering around in the wilderness. It was only the second month after their escape from Egypt. Already, the glorious vision of freedom had turned into the reality of hunger and thirst in an inhospitable land. And so they complained again, this time to Moses and Aaron. "If only we had died by the hand of the Lord in the land of Egypt, when we sat by the fleshpots and ate our fill of bread; for you have brought us out into this wilderness to kill this whole assembly with hunger" (Exod. 16:3). Freedom is a wonderful thing. But if you are starving to death, what good is it? Better to live as a well-fed slave than to die from hunger as a free person. Even slavery in Egypt began to look good compared to this. Human memory can be very short as their present situation transformed the horror of their past into the "good old days."

Humans cannot have hope if the basic necessities of life are not met. Lofty ideals like freedom and noble virtues like love and generosity are to be desired, but when one has nothing to eat, the need for food will take precedence over everything else.

If one cannot sustain life with sufficient food and water, then there is, obviously, no hope. Death will come, sooner rather than later, and that will be the end of it. The Israelites may sound ungrateful with their constant complaining about their situation (after all, God and Moses have just achieved their freedom), but they do reflect a human reality. Hope is not likely on an empty stomach.

God responds. Food will be provided. There will be quail in the evening and manna in the morning. (Later the people will complain again because they're getting bored with the same old menu. How many different ways can you prepare manna? See Num. 11:4-6.) And when necessary, Moses will be able to extract water from a rock (read Exod. 16:1-17:7 for more details). God hears our need for the everyday necessities of life, those things that we need for our bodies if we are to survive. People continue to pray to God for food, for sufficient rain, for abundant crops in the hope that God still listens and responds to such prayers as in ancient days in the wilderness.

When we attempt to revive hope in a despairing world, it is important to remember what should be done first. Without food, there is no hope. And so missionaries and church world relief agencies concern themselves first with providing the necessities of life. Then, later, people are able to hear and respond to the good news of the Gospel, the story of a God who knows all their needs and comes to meet them.

### 5. David's sins are forgiven (2 Sam. 12:13-14)

Without the possibility of forgiveness, hope can be very tenuous. Our relationships with both God and other people give us reason to hope. But what if we say or do the wrong thing, what if we commit some impulsive act of disobedience or hurt, what if we deeply offend both God and those whom we love? Will they, then, abandon us? We all know that such possibilities are always present. Or, the roles could be reversed. My spouse or children or best friend betrays my trust. I do not know if I am capable of forgiveness. Is my relationship gone? What will happen to my hope if this important resource is no longer available to me?

If forgiveness is not possible, hope is even more elusive than it need be. The possibility of forgiveness means that we can be free to make mistakes, to take action when we perceive that it is necesary. We can avoid the paralysis of inaction that is bound by fear of not doing the right thing. Forgiveness means that I can expect my relationships with God and loved ones to survive the normal (and sometimes above normal) stresses of daily life. God and I, my wife and I, my daughters and I, my best friend and I know that we have a future together. No matter what conflicts and differences we may have, forgiveness gives us the assurance that we are (and always will be) in this together.

The people of Israel remembered David as the greatest king they ever had. All kings who followed him were judged over against him and, with rare exceptions, fell far short of that standard. Solomon achieved greater glory and world renown. He built the temple, amassed wealth, and was known for his wisdom. Though they took pride in Solomon, he was not the model of the ideal king. Rather, they chose David.

They knew David was not perfect. In fact, they dared to tell stories about David's participation in murder, his act of adultery, his failure to control the lust and jealousy and ambition of his own sons. What made David great was his willingness to admit his sin and to seek forgiveness. When Nathan the prophet confronted him about his disgraceful sin with Bathsheba, he did not deny everything or say that he was the king and he could do what he darn well pleased or send Nathan's head home in a basket. The world has too few leaders who openly admit their wrongdoing and ask for our forgiveness. Maybe we would actually be moved to forgive if a politician or other person in authority surprised us by such an act of contrition.

David is forgiven (2 Sam. 12:13). His admission of guilt made the forgiveness possible. Psalm 51 has by tradition been associated with David's time of confession after the confrontation with Nathan (see the heading to Psalm 51). As we read this familiar psalm, often in the context of a formal liturgical service, we identify ourselves with David in our recognition that we are sinners in need of forgiveness and in our assurance that God is ready to forgive.

God is a God of forgiveness. That makes our relationship with God a source of hope even with the reality of human sin. As with David, even the worst of sins can be forgiven. But we are also reminded by the story of David, even forgiveness cannot remove all the consequences of our sin. By hurting others we may have set into motion problems that will continue even after forgiveness has been granted. Nathan tells David that troubles will continue in his family and, in fact, the child conceived with Bathsheba will die. Forgiveness has not changed that. Once forgiven, it is our responsibility to work to alleviate the results of the wrong that we have done. But we cannot fix all that has come from our misdeeds. This cold truth only intensifies our remorse and our need to be forgiven.

### 6. Habakkuk waits for the Lord (Hab. 1:13; 2:1-4)

The prophet Habakkuk has a serious question that he wants to take up with God. He is living in a dreadful time. The nation of Judah and the city of Jerusalem are about to be destroyed by the invading Babylonians. How could this happen to those special people with whom God had made a covenant to protect from all danger and to keep intact forever under the dynasty of the great king David? Other prophets had warned that such a fate might come to Judah if they did not change their ways. So, their destruction made some sense as punishment by a just God for their disobedience. But it seemed more complicated than that to Habakkuk. He has a question for God which implies some criticism of the way God is executing justice among the nations of the world. "Your eyes (he is speaking to God) are too pure to behold evil, and you cannot look on wrongdoing; why do you look on the treacherous and are silent when the wicked swallow those more righteous than they?" (Hab. 1:13). If God is just (as Habakkuk has just reminded him), then why should Judah be destroyed by people more wicked than they? You may make a case against Judah and point out all her sins, but her misdeeds are rather minor league compared to the enormous evils committed by the invaders from Babylon.

Human beings in need of hope often have questions about God's justice. Why should terrible things happen to good (or at least relatively good) people while wicked people prosper and go on committing atrocities against others? If God is not just, if the wicked will never be curtailed and punished, if the innocent are forever at their mercy, then where is the reason for hope? Is God at work in the world or not?

So how does God respond to the audacious question raised by the prophet? It is important to note that such questions are legitimate. The Bible abounds with challenges to God that may seem to our pious ears to be impertinent. But if the question is in our mind already, better to ask it than to let it smolder and inhibit our honest conversation with God. God does respond to such questions, as in this case. But God's answers are often indirect, providing a word that may be helpful but is not exactly on the point of the question that was asked. God does not explain to him why wicked Babylon should be used as a punishing rod against God's special people. Rather, God tells Habakkuk to wait in patience, trust, and hope. It is not time yet. But justice will come. Hang in there. Until the time when all the seeming injustices of the world are resolved, "the righteous live by their faith" (Hab. 2:4b). Sorry, Habakkuk, you asked for more, you wanted a precise and logical explanation, but, at least for now, this is all that you will get.

Is that enough for him? Does God's response satisfy him sufficiently that he can settle back and turn his waiting into hope? The final verses of the book seem to indicate that this is the case. "Though the fig tree does not blossom, and no fruit is on the vines; though the produce of the olive fails and the fields yield no food; though the flock is cut off from the fold and there is no herd in the stalls, yet I will rejoice in the Lord. I will exult in the God of my salvation" (Hab. 3:17-18).

Like many of us, Habakkuk does not have all his questions resolved. The world is filled with examples of suffering, injustice, and unmet human need that raise questions about God's intentions for our future. But, mysteriously, Habakkuk, and we too, go forward in hope. Hope is closely related to faith. And the righteous shall live by their faith.

### 7. Let Job say how bad it is (Job 7:6; 13:15a)

Job is a long and complicated book that discusses the problem of suffering at more length and in more depth than any other book in the Bible. The basic problem is that Job is a good man (even God brags about him in Job 1:8 and 2:3) but he has more trouble than anyone. If there is justice and fairness in the world, then people like Job should not have to endure such suffering. Is Job as innocent and undeserving as God has said, or are his friends right to insist that there must be some flaw in him that has brought on all of his calamities?

How does Job, himself, respond to the sudden disastrous turn in his life? Most of us have heard of the "patience" of Job. Already in the New Testament (see James 5:11) and throughout Christian history, Job has been presented as the one who bore his trials with endurance. This model is drawn primarily from the first 2 chapters of the book of Job, and it ignores the Job who compains bitterly about his situation from chapters 3 to 31. Job's willingness to bear his suffering stoically, with a stiff upper lip, without protest, has become the model for how a Christian should bear up under suffering. This demonstrates an interesting exercise in selective memory. What about the rest (in fact, the majority) of the book?

A typical expression from Job is found in 7:6. "My days are swifter than a weaver's shuttle, and come to their end without hope." He admits that hope has left him. Nothing makes sense anymore. He always tried to do the right thing but all these disasters came anyway. All his life he believed that God was a God of justice and power who could be trusted, but now he has even begun to doubt that. His family and friends (those who have not already died) have turned away from him in disgust. His friends are more interested in condemning him than in comforting him. We should not be surprised when he says that he has no hope.

In 13:15a, Job says, "See, he will kill me; I have no hope." This is a very strong statement. What hope is there if even God is out to kill us? Interestingly, some translations of this half verse, give us us a very different meaning: "Though he kill me, yet will I trust in him." Here, Job seems to be saying something similar to the end of Habakkuk. No matter how bad things get, he will continue to trust and (since the two go together) to hope. Though these translations are diametrically opposite, they can be explained rather easily by a close look at a minor change in the Hebrew text. The problem, then, is, which reading represents the real feeling, thoughts, and expression of Job—loss of hope or affirming hope in the face of anything that can happen? The pious translator often chooses the latter, even though it runs counter to almost everything else that Job is saying in this part of the book.

Will we let Job tell us honestly just how bad it is, how devastated he has become, how hopeless it all seems? Is there a place for such expressions of negativity in our search for a revival of hope? Though our religious tradition is uncomfortable with that idea and often tries to suppress the complaint, the doubt, the hard questions thrown to God, the mere presence of such material in the Bible gives them a legitimacy to which we should attend. It may seem strange, paradoxical, even illogical, but it is true that hope can actually be revived by the articulation of our hopelessness as long as there is someone to hear us. Particularly, this is true when the one who hears is God, himself. God does respond to our cries that we have no hope. We do not have to wait until hope returns before we can come to God with our concerns. God is ready to hear, right now, no matter in what state of spiritual disarray or intellectual confusion we find ourselves.

### 8. Dreams of peace for this world and beyond (Isa. 11:1-9)

We expect a lot from our government leaders. One of their primary tasks is to protect us from hostile aggressors. Wars and threats of war are always with us. By the time we have lived long enough, we can remember several times when we have been asked to switch our attitudes towards other countries. Nations that used to be our enemies have become our friends—and vice versa. But there always seems to be some enemy to fear. And so we judge our political leaders on how well they have kept the peace and prepared us to hold off any potential foe. Our goal is to preserve peace, though that often takes the form of preparing for war.

We also hold our leaders responsible for how well they maintain peace within our own country. Are they fair and even-handed, not giving special favors to a select few? Do they make sure that justice is available for all, not just for those with special status? Do they work hard to ensure that the basic needs of life are available to all citizens? We are always looking for the perfect leader—another George Washington or Abraham Lincoln or Winston Churchill (or Moses or David)—who will straighten out our messes and govern us so well that we can live together in peace and be secure about the future. We yearn for leaders in whom we can put our trust and pray that God will send them to us.

Where do we find such leaders, people who will make this world a better and safer place in which to live? In Isa. 11:1-5 the prophet looks backward for such a leader (as we often do in our search for the right model). It will be someone from the stump of Jesse and, therefore, from the house of David. With all his faults, David remained as the prime example of what a king should be. The new ruler from the line of David will be empowered by the Spirit of the Lord, will rule with equity over the poor and the meek, and will see that the wicked are destroyed. Our expectations for human rulers has not changed much over the years. Government officials with such traits are still much desired, even if rarely found.

But there is more going on in this prophetic passage than a longing, at last, to have some decent and effective human leadership. As desirable as that may be, it will not be enough. All human leaders will fall short. Wars have been present in every generation and that, no doubt, will continue. Our longing for peace and rest reaches beyond anything this world has to offer. God knows our needs for this life. We are not to belittle them as if they did not matter. But God also knows our deeper yearning for a peace that the world cannot give. Christians have seen in this Isa. 11 text a promise for a new king whose kingdom will not be of this world, who will outshine even the great David, himself.

Further, the Isa. 11 passage continues with a wonderful vision of what peace could be. In "the peaceable kingdom" even animals that are normally hostile to each other (who even eat each other) will lie down together in peace. God says, "They will not hurt or destroy on all my holy mountain" (Isa. 11:9a). A world like this is much different from the one that we know. Everything has been rearranged so that old hostilities are gone. The prophet asks us to expand our mind and imagine a new world where troubles are gone and our longing for peace and rest has been fully met.

Many biblical writers, as the prophet here in Isa. 11, come to God with the expectation that God will renew their hope for both this world and the next. God is concerned for both. This life should not be abandoned as hopeless, no matter how bad things get, as if God cannot or will not act, as if human existence is only a rehearsal for the real action that comes after we die. This life matters. But, thank God, it is not all that there is. The vision of the prophet into the mysteries beyond this life gives us a glimpse of God's ultimate intention for us.

### 9. A reality check for Jeremiah (Jer. 12:1-5)

Jeremiah is sometimes called the "crying prophet." To be sure, God had given him a very difficult assignment. He was called to warn the people of coming disaster if they did not mend their ways. Prophets of "bad news" are never popular. If they speak of decline and destruction when things are still going well, they are laughed off as hopeless pessimists, morbid misfits of society. If they continue to speak when the signs of impending doom can no longer be denied, they are somehow held responsible for the trouble. And so Jeremiah was forced to speak a messge he did not like to a people who did not want to hear it. He felt isolated, lonely, and persecuted, even by his own family and neighbors.

In his misery, Jeremiah often brought his complaint to God, and a number of his laments are preserved in his book. In 12:1-4 he objects to the injustice that he sees everywhere. The wicked and treacherous thrive while he, the just one on a crusade commissioned by God, has endured all kinds of misery. It's time for God to do something, to rise up and act, to live up to God's reputation for justice. To be blunt, Jeremiah asks God to "pull them out like sheep for the slaughter and set them apart for the day of slaughter"

(12:3b). That may not be a nice thing for Jeremiah to say, but he sees the pain and suffering that wicked people are inflicting on the nation and he wonders why God doesn't do something. And also, lest we be too hard in judging Jeremiah's hostility, we must remember the awful suffering that he himself has endured. Unless God does something, the whole country, and he personally, will continue to suffer.

So how does God respond to this plea for immediate justice against the wicked? Perhaps we would expect to hear a consoling, soothing word of encouragement from God. Maybe God will speak softly and tell Jeremiah how appreciative he is that Jeremiah has taken on this tough job. But God is just as blunt as Jeremiah had been and says, "If you have raced with foot-runners and they have wearied you, how will you compete with horses? And if in a safe land you fall down, how will you fare in the thickets of the Jordan?" (12:5). In short, "You ain't seen nothin' yet, Jeremiah." This is not quite what Jeremiah wanted when he came to God looking for a word of hope.

God does not always respond to our need for hope in ways that we expect. Sometimes the word from God may sound unnecessarily harsh, even critical. But it still may be a word of hope. God has heard and responded. It is better to hear the truth from God than a premature and shallow optimism that cannot provide the strength to face the trials that still lie ahead.

With regard to God's response to this specific lament from Jeremiah, we should note a number of things that could help us if ever in similar circumstances. (a) God does not want to destroy and is never in a hurry to eliminate people, even those we are quick to classify as wicked and beyond redemption. (b) Though we probably (it is hoped) will never be given a task as unpleasant as Jeremiah's, it is possible that God may ask us to take on a mission that will require some sacrifice from us. Whoever said that it would be easy to follow God (Jesus certainly didn't say that)? (c) At this point in our life, there may be no relief from the suffering. In fact, as in Jeremiah's case, it might even get worse before it gets better. (d) But there will be an end to it, finally. And, in the meantime, God will provide the protection necessary to carry on.

This promise occurs several times in Jeremiah, as in 15:20—"And I will make you to this people a fortified wall of bronze; they will fight against you, but they shall not prevail over you, for I am with you to save you and deliver you, says the Lord."

### 10. The long wait is almost over (Rom. 8:18-25)

Paul, like earlier biblical writers, had to deal with the impatience of God's people as they waited for God to act to complete what had been started, to remove all obstacles to hope, to bring peace and justice and prosperity and happiness once and for all. Paul, as other followers of Jesus, believed that the Messiah had come. The long expected savior of the world had entered history in the person of Jesus of Nazareth. But not much had changed. Violence, war, unjust rulers, disease, grief, poverty, and death were still present just as they had always been. In fact, there was now even more suffering for those who were willing to stand up and make a public witness about Jesus. Further, the world of nature was still unreliable and capricious. Some years there was not enough rain and other years brought floods. Strong winds and hail often destroyed the crops just before harvest. Earthquakes were not uncommon. So how have things actually improved since the Messiah came? Surely he will have to come again to complete the task of saving the world.

In the wonderful eighth chapter of Romans, Paul addresses a number of these concerns. This chapter is filled with one treasure after another. For now, let us concentrate on words of assurance and hope in 8:18-25.

The suffering of the present time is not worth comparing with the glories that are to come (v. 18). Though the present troubles are real, hard, awful, tragic, they will pale into insignifance in light of the glorious future that God has in store for us.

It has been a long wait, not only for individual people but for the world as a whole. The whole creation has been groaning in labor pains until now (v. 22). Paul uses this imagery of pregnancy and birth to talk about the agony of waiting. It is like a pregnancy that has gone on for decades since Jesus, centuries since Abraham and Moses, and millenia since the sin of our first parents. And we later day Christians can now add a couple more millenia to the time of waiting. That is a very long pregnancy. No wonder the expectant parents are a little impatient.

When the change for which we have all been longing and groaning finally occurs, it will be radical, monumental, virtually impossible for mere mortals to imagine. It is not only people that will change, but the whole creation. It will be so glorious that the present suffering is inconsequential by comparison. The "peaceable kingdom" of Isa. 11:6-9 tries to capture some of the radicality of this new world with its picture of formerly hostile creatures docily co-existing.

In spite of this long wait (and it always seems long to those who wait), Paul speaks with a sense of immediacy. The time of fulfillment is coming soon. It won't be much longer. Just hang in there. And as we wait, we have the advantage of possessing the first fruits of the Spirit (v. 23). We are not waiting as those who have no reason to hope. We have the whole record of God's efforts to reach out and redeem the fallen human race. We know what kind of God this is. We know the story of Jesus—who he was and how he lived and what he taught and how he died and how he rose again. We have these signs of God working in the world, assurances that God's promises will be kept, evidence that things will change and the time is not far off.

But it is surely further off than Paul had thought. Many generations of Christians have come and gone since these words were mailed to the Romans. But since we still must wait we continue to be comforted and strengthened by Paul's words. His witness helps us to hope as we wait.

## C. Hope for What? (The content of hope)

What do we want as we look forward to the future? What is on our "wish list?" What do we need (or think we need) if our future is to be good? In this section we will look at some items that would likely be on most people's lists. In our desire for them, we are in harmony with our biblical ancestors. Mostly, they represent things that God has promised us. Perhaps we have misread some of those promises. Maybe we have not heard them fully. Maybe we have expected too much from <u>this</u> life. Possibly
we have placed too much emphasis on the <u>what</u> of our hope, almost as if (either consciously or uncounsciously) we were putting God to the test. If we have not received that for which we had hoped, we are tempted to lose confidence in God's promises to provide and, thus, our hope is in jeopardy.

Can hope survive such crises as this? Yes, if we are able to renew a relationship of trust in God in spite of failure to achieve certain specific hopes, and if we have a hope that is able to see beyond all earthly limitations.

### 1. Food, water, and a place to live (Ps. 145:15-16)

The drought in that part of South Dakota had been excessively severe that year. It had not rained for several months. The pastor of the local church decided that it was time for a prayer meeting. Had not God promised to provide rain and crops, to give us our daily bread? He still remembered the prayer before meals when he was a boy: "The eyes of all look to you, and you give them their food in due season. You open your hand, satisfying the desire of every living thing" (Ps. 145:15-16). Prayer meetings were not common in his denomination's tradition, but these were desperate times. Nothing else had worked. His plan was to involve as many of the congregation as possible, especially the farmers, in the prayers. When he talked to Ray Johnson, he got a firm "No." The pastor felt that his reluctance was more than the usual reticence to say anything, especially a prayer, in public. Finally, Ray let it out. "You know it won't do any good, Pastor, until the wind changes direction."

Do we still come to God with confidence asking for rain, for good crops, food for the hungry, shelter for the homeless? Do we still believe that God will provide these basic necessities of life? There is much in the Bible about this as semi-nomad people wandered from place to place looking for pasture and/or places to settle down and plant crops. They expressed their hopes to God and God promised to give them a land, food, and prosperity. The possession of land became a sign of God's promise and loss of it an indication of God's punishment.

Most of us are insulated from these basic needs as more and more of us live in cities and suburbs in a prosperous part of the world. Yet, if we pay attention, we continue to hear about droughts, floods, loss of jobs and income (and, therefore food and shelter), the bankruptcy of the family farm, homeless people on the streets, refugees throughout the world, and long-standing disputes over the land in places like Ireland, Palestine, and the Balkan peninsula.

These needs are so basic that they override all other hopes. Obviously, without food and water, one will die. And so, without these things, at least as far as this world is concerned, there is no hope. We cannot make it rain or hold back the flood or send the warmth of the sun at just the right time to ripen the fruit, and we may wonder sometimes why God does not regulate those things a bit better. But there are things that we can, and are expected, to do to meet these human needs—to feed the hungry, provide shelter for the homeless, see that the wealth of the earth is shared in at least some measure of equity. Moses and the prophets and Jesus have all reminded us of these responsibilities. God still wants to fulfill these hopes for people and expects us to co-operate with him to see that it is done. Further, we are called to work to settle land disputes between warring nations, some of which are supported by conflicting understandings of the land as a gift from God. With regard to this area of human need, God depends on human participation to provide what is needed and, thereby, to renew human hope.

And we need to remember that, as important as these necessities are for life and hope, they can also become symbols for a hope that goes even beyond earthly need. Hope is still a possibility even when tragedy, starvation, famine, and homelessness remain. We do not live by bread alone and Jesus becomes the bread of life. Jesus tells us to come to drink of the living water, which is more than the deepest, purest well can provide. And when we die, we are promised a heavenly home, not in Palestine, but across the Jordan into the new Jerusalem.

### 2. Protection from danger (Ps. 27:1)

As we look into the future, we can see many things that have the potential to hurt us. There is the big picture: wars that start small but then take on a life of their own, destruction of resources and pollution of the environment, crime in the streets and corruption in government, the state of the economy, poverty and homelessness and inadequate health care. These issues will have direct implications on individual lives, though not equally on all. We also worry about threats to our individual security. Will we and our family avoid serious illness and live to a comfortable old age? Will we be safe when we walk home at night in our own neighborhood? Will the plane take off and land as it is supposed to? Will the drunk drivers on the highway stay away from our car? Each new day is an adventure into the unknown as we step out the door into a dangerous world. (Of course, it's not safe to stay home, either, because, as is often said, "Most accidents occur at home.")

We have learned from our religious tradition to trust that God will protect us from danger. Many of the psalms ask God for protection before a journey and thank God after returning home safely (e.g., Ps. 121). Some speak more generally of God's overall protection (as Ps. 27:1—"The Lord is my light and my salvation, whom shall I fear? The Lord is the stronghold of my life; of whom shall I be afraid?") The Bible contains stories of God's active presence with those in great peril (e.g., the Hebrew people in Egypt and in the wilderness or Daniel in the lions' den). Following their example, we pray to God that the diagnosis will be benign, the operation will be a success, the trip will be free of hazards, our children living far from us will be safe. God has promised to answer prayers like that.

But how well does it work? How much does God interfere in the specifics of human lives? Does God keep the airplane engine from failing, change the direction of the oncoming vehicle, guide the surgeon's hand, keep us away from the street where the muggers are lurking? People will respond to such questions in different ways, depending on how they understand the way God works in the world and conditioned by their own experience.

Some will testify with great confidence, perhaps even write books, about how God acted in their lives to save them from a terrible danger. They become witnesses to all of us that God does indeed act within this world in particular ways to enhance our safe journey through life. All of us would like to believe that. But some have difficulty harmonizing that belief with tragedies that they have seen, some of which may have touched them intimately. They ask, "Why me? Where was God when I (or my spouse or daughter or parent) needed protection?" Or, sometimes one who has been saved from a situation where others have perished puts a different slant on the "Why me?" question. The sole survivor from a fire, or an airline crash, or an automobile accident, carries a different kind of burden. They may give thanks for survival, but wonder about the lack of protection for those who died and be confused about what to do to justify their own escape.

Those who have been tested by what seems to be a lack of protection from God may become cynical about God's involvement in the day to day events of life. To be sure, we need to face these hard questions with humility and a sense for the mystery of life, but we should fight back against an attitude that removes God completely from participation in our daily lives. Some day, all will be resolved. In the meantime, the words of Paul at the end of Romans 8 are a good reminder that if God is for us, there is no enemy powerful enough to harm us. Though within this earthly life, in spite of God's protection, we are still vulnerable to hurt, pain, and suffering, there is nothing in heaven or on earth that can destroy us completely or "separate us from the love of God in Christ Jesus our Lord" (Rom. 8:39).

## 3. That the good will remain and the bad will go away ( Eccles. 12:1-8; Job 1:5)

If a person has a good life, loving relationships, robust health, rewarding work, then hope will not require any radical changes. In fact, the very opposite may be true. If one already has all that he or she ever wanted, then hope takes the form of opposition to change. Assaults on hope for such a person will come from the knowledge that all things change, nothing stays the way that it is forever, and this is probably too good to last. Sometimes, for the sake of hope, these people will fight against change, hanging on as best they can for as long as possible to what they already have.

For others, there is no hope unless things change, perhaps even in radical ways. People living under oppression in totalitarian countries, slaves living in shacks in the American South, those suffering from chronic and debilitating illnesses, or the person in the midst of a terrible depression can be hopeful only if they can be assured that the present state of existence will not continue forever. If there is no hope for change throughout one's earthly life, they will long for an afterlife in which the terrible ordeals of this existence will be replaced by what is new and glorious and different (as in the beautiful images of heaven in the Negro Spirituals).

For some, hope means that nothing will change. For others, it means that everything must change. The Old Testament Wisdom literature provides us good examples of these contrasting expectations for the future.

The writer of Ecclesiastes has had everything. He was a respected leader, renowned for his wisdom, and his wealth gave him the means to enjoy the best that life had to offer. Apparently, his life had sailed along rather nicely with no great trauma or suffering. But now he was getting old, and he realized that, as good as it had been, it was all going to end pretty soon. And he was having a hard time finding any permanent meaning to his life. All he had acquired would be squandered by future generations and he would be forgotten. Change was coming, whether he liked it or not. He could not hold on to the past. If this life was all that there was (as he seemed to believe), then there was no hope. One should live it up while still young enough to enjoy it, because the days of old age are coming all too soon, and finally, death (see especially Eccles. 12:1-8).

Job, too, had had a wonderful life filled with respect, wealth, wisdom, a loving family. He, too, no doubt hoped that none of this would change, though he had some fear that it might and he did all that he could to keep things as they were (see Job 1:5). Sure enough, his worst fears materialized (and more). In a series of terrible disasters, he lost everything, including his children. Whereas he had previously hoped that nothing would change, now his only hope was that things would change. He almost lost hope, in despair that he was doomed to this misery for the rest of his life, and he had little hope for an afterlife. But here and there appeared some glimmers of hope. Maybe God would still listen to him, restore his good name, rebuild his broken family, and restore all that he had lost. And all this did come about.

We all need hope. Those who seem to be the lucky ones who cruise through life winning all the prizes and enjoying every day need hope. Change is inevitable and, without hope, fear of change can be devastating to those who have been given much. And clearly, those who have suffered through life, who have had their Job-like experiences, need to know that their present situation, no matter how unchangeable and permanent it seems, is not the end of the story.

Whether life has been good to us or has presented us with more than our share of burdens, we all need hope.

### 4. Friends, counselors, human support

"If there is any encouragement in Christ, any consolation from love, any sharing in the Spirit, any compassion and sympathy, make my joy complete: be of the same mind, having the same love, being in full accord and of one mind" (Philip. 2:1-2).

The presence (or absence) of close human relationships will have an enormous effect on one's ability to hope. We would consider anyone who preferred to face the future alone, without the loving support of other people, to be peculiar. Most of us take hope in the thought that someone will be there with us to share the good and to bring us consolation when things go badly. When something wonderful happens to us, we look for someone with whom to share the news. We almost burst with our story until we can blurt it out and see the happiness on the face of our loved one or friend. When we are confronted with disappointment, an illness, or grief, we also look for another to hear us and be with us. The old platitude is true: "Misery loves company."

We hope that no matter what comes into our life—good or bad—someone will be there. We want the security that certain key relationships in our lives will be so lasting and reliable that they will survive whatever crises may occur. Words like "commitment" and "forgiveness" are very important for such hopes to be realistic and not merely romantic or sentimental ideals. Unfortunately, in these days, many fear commitment and want to keep relationships flexible enough so that one can easily move out when the going gets rough. And forgiveness is often overshadowed by the desire to get even and never forget the hurt. Those who do not have intimate relationships with others long for them. Those who have them, pray they will continue.

But even those who love us, whose intention is to support us, who do not waver in their commitment to us, sometimes respond to our joy and pain in ways different from what we had hoped. When we speak to share our success, we may be surprised by our friend's indifference, as if he does not realize what a wonderful thing this is. Or, sometimes, we even note a touch of envy, so that we are almost sorry that we mentioned it. He reacts to our expression of happiness as if we were boasting and unfairly comparing our accomplishments with his. It is not always easy to share in another's success, even when we want to.

In times of deep trouble, we particularly need the loving assurance of others. Again, even those with whom we have close, long-term relationships, sometimes react in ways that are not helpful, that do not meet our expectations of what we would like from them. When confronted by suffering in friends or family, people are often uncomfortable and bewildered, feeling helpless and hopeless. Like Job's friends, who came with the intention of bringing comfort, they sometimes act in ways that have a quite different effect.

They may hide from unpleasantness by avoiding the suffering person, with the excuse that they are too busy. Or, when actually sitting in the same room, they are careful to keep the conversation on small talk, changing the subject when the sufferer wants to express painful and confusing thoughts and feelings. Or they may try to say too much, to talk before listening, to offer explanations for the sufferer's predicament that may not be appropriate, helpful, true, or kind. Some ways of understanding suffering put the blame on the sufferer, herself, and a well-meaning comforter who suggests such possibilities may be heard as condemnatory, not as a renewer of hope.

What most of us need as we face low points in our life is a loving person (or persons) who will not hide from us, even if we behave badly and lash out in anger or despair because of our misery. We are mostly concerned that this person will simply be there to listen, and we are less eager to hear intellectualizing about what all this means. We want someone who will stay with us, forgive us, comfort us, and not leave us to face the future alone. Whether experiencing joy or confronting sorrow, we long for human relationships that will nourish, sustain, and enlarge our hope. And we pray that we can be such messengers of hope to others. "We love because he first loved us. . . The commandment we have from him is this: Those who love God must love their brothers and sisters also" (1 John 1:19, 21).

### 5. God's presence as forgiver, not condemner (Ps. 139:1-12)

When we say good-bye to someone, we are really uttering a shortened version of "God be with you." We hope that God will be present in their lives as we part from one another. We do not believe in a God who set the world in motion by a fantastic act of creativity and then went off into another corner of the universe to contemplate other projects. If God is to fulfill our hopes for the necessities of life, protection from danger, a moral world, and assurance in our times of despair, then God must be present. We do not want a God who in an absentee landlord, who set up a system that runs automatically on a supernatural computer, and now lives someplace else where he cannot be reached when something needs to be fixed. We believe, we hope, in a God who is with us, whose name is "Immanuel."

Those who have endured hard times in their life tell us that they sometimes feel as if God has abandoned them. The Psalmist (and, later, Jesus) says, "My God, my God, why have you forsaken me?" (Ps. 22:1). Job wants to argue with God about the injustice of his situation but he does not know where to find God—"Oh, that I knew where I might find him" (Job. 23:3a). The feeling that God is absent can be a terrifying experience. At the very time when God's loving presence and a reassuring word is most needed, God seems inaccessible. And so, in hope, we pray that God will always be with us as we go into the future and that God will let us know that he is there.

But it is not enough to be aware of God's presence. We need to know that the God who is present in our lives is much more interested in forgiveness than in condemnation or punishment. The mere statement of God's presence can send mixed messages. If God is present, then why doesn't God do something to take away the troubles, the pain, the violence, the suffering? Does God not care? Or, if God is present and at work in what is happening to me, that may mean that God is causing my trouble as punishment for something I have done. How am I to regard this God who is personally involved in the unpleasantness in my life? Is this ever present God on my side or not? If not, then maybe I would be better off with a God who kept his distance.

Psalm 139 is a beautiful statement of God's continued presence, no matter where we go or what happens to us. Even if we should flee up to heaven or down to Sheol or off to the farthest limits of the sea, "even there your hand shall lead me, and your right hand shall hold me fast" (Ps. 139:10). Most people read this as a comforting, hope-producing word about God's promise to be with us always no matter what. It is a promise similar to Paul's assurance that nothing can separate us from the love of God (Rom. 8:38-39).

But in times of deep trouble, when hope wanes and trust in God is shaken, even the assurance of God's presence can take a negative turn. Amos knows Psalm 139 and he turns it upside down. It becomes a word about God's decision to destroy those who have been disobedient, who have thought they could get away with it because God was not present, not watching, and not acting. No matter where they go to hide—from deepest Sheol to highest heaven to the bottom of the sea—God will find them, not to bring them good but to punish them (Amos 9:2-4). Similarly, Job, who longed for a face to face audience with God (in Job 23), also had his moments when he wished God would go away and leave him alone. If God would quit picking on him and get off his back, he could have at least a moment of peace (Job 7:12-21).

And so our hope is for God's presence as we move into the unknown future. Further, we pray for assurance that God will always be on our side, slow to anger, quick to forgive, always working toward what is good. With that assurance, we can dare to hope.

### 6. Justice, a moral world

"The earth is given into the hand of the wicked; he (God) covers the eyes of its judges—if it is not he, who then is it?" (Job 9:24).

Children (like Job in this passage) seem to come equipped with a low tolerance for injustice. "It isn't fair," is one of the most common complaints that parents hear from their offspring. In exasperation, mothers and fathers have been known to respond in a cynical tone, "Who said the world is supposed to be fair?" But we do want the world to be fair. There is a deep longing in the human heart for good to be rewarded and evil punished, for right to prevail over wrong, for the story to have a happy ending. We want that to be true so that we can have some evidence that God is at work in the world and that God is just, so that we can have some basis on which to make moral choices, so that we can have a reason to delay immediate gratification or even take on some sacrifice. We want our world to have some order and meaning.

God is a God of justice. We have put our trust in a God who has set up rules of morality and holds us to them. Sin and disobedience will not be tolerated. Violation of God's specific commands will lead to unpleasant consequences. God did not wish it to turn out that way. God does not want to punish, but God's justice demands accountability. Permissiveness only leads to further violations of God's law. And so the Bible contains the story of the fall of humanity (Gen. 3), the law codes with their warnings of curse or promises of blessing, the history of Israel as an example of disaster that comes from disobedience, and the Proverbs with their sometimes simplistic connection between deed and consequence.

But our insistence on God's justice can lead us into difficulties. We may attempt to explain the suffering of every individual as a result of their own sin and forget that sometimes evil people hurt those who are innocent or the suffering may have another cause or remain a mystery. We may naively expect God's justice to work without any glitches in a world still ridden with sin and, therefore, complain about God's lack of justice when the real problem may be with ourselves and other human beings. Or we can become so tormented with the suffering of the innocent that we surrender to despair about God's lack of involvement or care. Or we may develop such a sense of perfectionism or scrupulousness that we fear God's punishment (both temporal and, especially, eternal), knowing we cannot possibly meet God's exalted standards. Or we can become so preoccuppied with the prosperity of the wicked that we feed our hostility and take delight in the misfortunes of others.

In spite of these difficulties, our hope for justice—both in this world and the next—continues to be a very important item on our list of things for which we hope. In this world, we are overwhelmed with examples of injustice, some perpetrated by us and some in which we are the victims. It is our task as followers of a just God to work with God to bring as much justice as humanly possible into this world that God loves and for which Christ died. By doing so, we help to renew hope in a world that desperately needs it.

As Christians, we continue to hope for a new age when God's justice will finally be achieved in its fullness. For us, that will be a time of promise and not dread. Though we know we are sinners, though we know God is just, we have no fear of condemnation or eternal punishment. God's justice is not the last word about God, but is always tempered with mercy and forgiveness. If justice must insist on some penalty for sin, that has already been paid. Good will win. Evil will be defeated. The faithful will be declared just by a loving God. Our hope is eternally secure.

### 7. To be remembered well (Job 19:23-27)

Jim Thorpe was one of the greatest athletes that America ever produced. He excelled in a number of sports and won several medals at the Olympic Games at the beginning of the twentieth century. Unfortunately, his medals were taken from him when it was discovered that he had received a few dollars for playing baseball. In an age when professional basketball players who make millions of dollars a year can play in the Olympics, it is hard to believe that Thorpe was deprived of his accomplishments for a sum barely adequate to pay for his lunch. For many years afterwards, even after his death, his children worked hard to restore his medals, his records, his status, his good name. How their father would be remembered was very important to them.

Before they are in office more than a couple of years, presidents of the United States begin to worry about what the historians will say about them. They are particularly anxious about this if things are not going too well for them at the moment. At least they hope to be appreciated by future generations. (Harry Truman is a classic example of a president whom everyone loves now but was one of the least popular presidents ever while still in office.) It has become the custom for retired presidents to set up their own libraries, not only to aid the research of writers of history and biography, but so that the ordinary tourist can come by and remember the great leader. It is important to be remembered—and remembered well.

When someone retires, the whole office gathers and an official person says something nice about the retiree. Maybe there will be brief words of praise engraved on a watch or a plaque. Even the epitaphs that some people choose to put on their tombstones are meant to remind the passerby (and the surviving kin) who this person was and how well they were regarded—"a good father," "a loving husband," "a friend to all," "greatly missed."

In the midst of his despair and hopelessness, Job still hoped that someone would stand up and remind everyone that he was a good man, he had suffered unfairly, he was not a bad sinner who deserved all this. If there was no human being who would stand up and make the case for his decency and accomplishments, maybe God, himself, would do it (Job 19:23-27). Though Job was not very confident that there was a life after death in which the injustices of this life could be rectified, he hoped that his good name would be remembered and honored—even if the vindication did not come until after he had died.

It is important to be remembered at all. We do not want to disappear off the face of the earth with no one around to recall who we were and how important we were to them and how our life had purpose and meaning. There is a kind of immortality in being remembered well. It is a way to live on in the hearts and minds of those whom we leave behind when we die. It brings a satisfaction and sense of completeness to our life. This is a common human need and a source of hope. It is not the same as hope for a life that continues after death. For those who do not live with that hope, it becomes even more important. But even for those of us who live within the promise of the resurrection, the desire to be remembered well is very strong.

On the human level, to know that others will remember us well strengthens our hope for the future. But, most of all, we wish for God to remember us, to know who we are and to think well of us. As followers of Jesus, we should have that assurance. The parts of our life which we would prefer to forget will pass quickly before God's eyes as God chooses to remember what is good.

### 8. If what we hoped for doesn't come (2 Cor. 12:7-10)

We have been looking at the object of our hopes, the things <u>for</u> which people hope. Very often we think of hope primarily in terms of the thing that we hope <u>for</u>. Our ability to hope is too closely tied to the fulfillment of the specific agenda that we have constructed in our minds. We want the necessities of life, protection from danger, human love and friendship, God's forgiving presence, a just and moral world, the legacy of a good reputation, and more. But, clearly, we do not receive everything for which we hope. Some of our prayers come up empty and our hopes unfulfilled. What do we do then? Do we go through a faith crisis? Do we question whether God has the power and will to keep his promises? Can our relationship of trust (and hope) survive the disappointment?

Paul provides us a good model of a person of faith who has experienced a negative answer to his prayer and has come to the realization that this particular hope will never be achieved. Paul tells us that he had a thorn in the flesh. There has been endless conjecture about what this might have been. Whatever it was, Paul very much wanted to be rid of it. Perhaps it caused him embarrassment, or pain, or limited his effectiveness, or gave people a wrong impression about him. Paul could argue with God that it should be removed not only for Paul's own sake, but for the sake of the work that he had undertaken. As successful as Paul had been in spreading the Gospel, just think what he could do if God would take away this impediment. Three times Paul came to God with this request. The answer was "no." But it was not just a flat "no," without a further word. God says, "My grace is sufficient for you, for my power is made perfect in weakness" (2 Cor. 12:9).

A few lessons from Paul for times when we experience frustrated hopes and seemingly unanswered prayers:

(a) Sometimes the answer is "no." We will not receive everything for which we hope. Not in this world, anyway. And we are in good company in that regard. To Paul's name, we could add Moses, David, Jeremiah, Job, and Jesus (who hoped the cup of pain could pass him by) to our list of major characters from the Bible who were sometimes denied that for which they hoped.

(b) God did answer, even though the word was not the one Paul hoped to hear. An answer is better than no answer. The relationship does go on. The failure to achieve all that was desired does not mean that God has left or is not interested or not compassionate about the problem that remains with Paul (or with us). God reminds Paul that he is a recipient of God's grace, and that is sufficient for the present time. Paul wanted more, but this is what he gets. And God says it is enough.

(c) Paul learns a lesson in humility. One key component of humility is the recognition that there are some things that happen in life that are beyond our control, that cannot be changed, and we must accommodate ourselves to that fact if we are to move ahead and not remain bitter and preoccuppied with what is impossible.

(d) Paul achieves a new insight about God's use of human weakness. The truth of the Gospel does not depend on our charm, our good looks, our eloquence, our gifts of clear thinking, our wonderful piety. God can use less than perfect people to spread the Gospel (a wonderful word of encouragement for us who have entered ordained ministry). We all have our own version of a "thorn in the flesh" which, we might argue, hinders us from being as effective disciples as we would like to be. This experience of Paul reminds us that God is with us to maximize our talents and minimize our defects as we seek to serve God as we are.

Hope can continue even though specific hopes are denied. God is still at work in our lives. We may even come to new and marvelous knowledge about God and ourselves and our role in life through our dissappointments.

## D. Hope in whom (or in what)?

Who (or what) is worthy of our hope? Are there any persons so reliable, so wise, so caring, that I would dare to place my future in their hands? Are there systems of government, economics, education, family, philosophy, medical care, which are dependable and in which I can invest my hope? If human beings and earthly systems fail me, is there a God who can be trusted so completely that I can happily turn over my life to divine providence? Perhaps, we need to distinguish those things in which we hope on the human level from our trust in God. So, we can trust human institutions and relationships and systems up to a point, but, in the ultimate sense, only God is completely worthy of our trust.

Most of the following are expressed in negative terms. They are worthy of our hope, more or less, for the time being, but we will be in serious trouble if we pin all our hopes on the things of this world. Where we choose to put our hope raises the age-old question of idolatry. There is only one God, and we are to have no other gods before him. To hope, without qualification, in anything other than the God of Israel and our Lord Jesus Christ, is to be perilously close to idolatry and to be vulnerable to the smashing of false hopes.

### 1. Not in things of this world (1 Cor. 15:19)

How do we find a proper balance between hope for this world and the realization that all things earthly have their limitations and cannot provide lasting hope? If we are too trusting, too naive about the altruism and wisdom of authority figures, too dependent on family or friends, too accepting of political ideologies as absolute truth for all time, then we run the risk of a severe letdown if and when these areas of hope do not meet our expectations. On the other hand, we do not wish to go through life with a cynical, negative attitude, unwilling to commit to any cause or trust any person because of potential flaws and the certainty that no one or nothing can be trusted completely. That view is too one-sided, too pessimistic, too morbid, perhaps too obsessed with the doctrine of universal sin. Such skepticism about the trustworthiness of anything earthly may sometimes be the consequence of experiences in which one has, in fact, been hurt or betrayed by those in whom hope had been placed.

We ought not to be too quick to reject this world. Christians have sometimes been accused of being much more interested in the world to come than in the one in which they presently live. God has put us here to enjoy the creation and to live in loving and responsible relationships with others and with the creation itself. On the human level, some persons and some systems are better than others. We need discernment to choose wisely where we should put our hope. We should have a healthy skepticism about some alternatives and considerable confidence in others.

But, in the final say, all earthly things will pass, change, disappear. Our relationships will not remain the same through all stages of life, governments will come and go, nations (even our own) will not last forever. If we wait long enough, even mountains will be worn down and continents will shift. The bottom line is the certainty that all of us will die. That is the cold reality. As Jesus said, "Heaven and earth will pass away, but my words will not pass away" (Matt. 24:35). So everything is transitory except the words, the promises, from God. In the face of a world that cannot provide the hope that we need, we are still able to turn to the God who can be trusted and to rest in his promises.

A person with a terminal illness struggles with how long to keep hoping for this world and when to turn oneself over to God and go hopefully into the unknown of death and what lies beyond. Most people want to hang onto this life as long as possible. Maybe there will be a miracle. Maybe we can muster up enough faith to bring about a reversal of the illness that will astound the doctors. The family does not want to let the loved one go. Maybe we can have a few more months or weeks or days of time together. Maybe there is still some unfinished business we need to do. We are often told that the will to live is what keeps one going, and we ought not to submit to the inevitability of death too soon. How long to continue the fight? How soon to acquiesce? Those questions are not easily answered.

The things of this world are to be cherished and enjoyed as precious gifts from God. We should never belittle them. But they are not sources of hope in the ultimate sense. With regard to this life, David said, when receiving offerings that would go into the temple, "For we are aliens and transients before you (God), as were all our ancestors; our days on the earth are like a shadow, and there is no hope" (1 Chron. 29:15). In the fifteenth chapter of 1 Corinthians, Paul discusses at some length his musings on what life after death might be. He makes a close connection between the resurrection of Jesus and our own rebirth after death. If either one of these is not true, then the other is not true either. And, he says, "If for this life only we have hoped in Christ, we are of all people most to be pitied" (1 Cor. 15:19). But pity is not necesary because our hope is not only for this world, but in the God who continues forever no matter what this world might bring.

### 2. Not in power or might (Ps. 33:16-17)

In order to ensure a safe and good future, nations seek to be strong enough to hold off any potential enemy. This usually means building up storehouses of arms, making alliances with our friends (some of whom may live on the doorstep of those nations we fear), and sometimes stifling protesting opinion within our own country. Then the supposed enemy sees what we are doing and decides that they must prepare to meet the threat that we represent to them. We see their response as a hostile act and increase our preparation for war—and the cycle goes on and on. In order to protect ourselves from danger, we may well have made ourselves more susceptible to what we most feared.

Often those who protest such activities are accused of being unrealistic, soft-headed, cowardly, pacifists, or, even traitors. If so, they are in good company with many biblical characters, who also were the target of such derogatory accusations. Samuel warned the Israelites, who were desperate to defend themselves from the invading Philistines, about the danger of giving too much power to an earthly king and abandoning their trust in God (1 Sam. 8). Isaiah warned about the folly of running down to Egypt to make alliances with someone like the Pharaoh rather than to look to the Holy One of Israel (Isa. 31:1). Jeremiah suggested that it is God's intention to punish Judah, so any efforts to try to hold off the Babylonians would be futile. Psalm 33:16-17 sums up the frequent biblical critique of trusting too much in power or might: "A king is not saved by his great army; a warrior is not delivered by his great strength. The war horse is a vain hope for victory, and by its great might it cannot save."

Again, we face the dilemma of where to put our hopes within the framework of this world, even if we grant that our ultimate salvation is dependent only on God. A few suggestions:

(a) Pacifism is not necesarily the answer, though some may follow their conscience into that position. Most of us would recognize the reality of evil and concede that sometimes it must be resisted, even if that leads us into war and violence. We are not to surrender to genuine evil. Unfortunately, wars are not usually fought between pure good and pure evil (though the Nazi menace came very close to unambiguous evil).

(b) The real issue is a matter of trust, as the biblical passages point out. Do we trust Pharaoh or God? Do we trust our war horses, tanks, planes, and bombs, or do we trust God? Has our passion for self-protection taken on the characteristics of a religion, all-consuming, and immune to criticism from those who see where it may be leading? Military preparedness may be a necessary compromise with the reality of a sinful world, but it becomes dangerous if it takes on a life of its own and too much hope is invested in it.

(c) There are other ways to work for peace besides power, coercion, suppression, control. Jesus did not come with power and might to change the world, but rather refused to fight back when the forces of religion and government rose up against him. On the personal level, within families and among friends, we may see a glimmer of how that might work, as people are changed through love and acceptance and not by force. Even there it will not always work. And in disputes between nations it is very hard to transfer a willingness to die for the other into any kind of meaningful national policy. Nevertheless, the example of Jesus (and a few people like Gandhi and Martin Luther king, Jr.) should at least make us uncomfortable with violence as a solution and give us a vision of other possibilities.

(d) Within history, there will always be wars and rumors of war. The peace envisioned by the prophets (both Isa. 2:2-4 and Mic. 4:1-4), where weapons of war have been converted to plowshares and pruning hooks, may be more an image of heaven than anything possible on earth. But that does not excuse us from efforts to work for as much peace as possible, occasionally resorting to shows of power, but in the knowledge that the ultimate goal will never be achieved by such means.

### 3. Not in the "system" (John 16:33; 18:36a)

If a human society is to thrive with a feeling of well-being and hope among its citizens, certain "systems" must function efficiently and fairly. There is little reason for hope if people begin to lose confidence in key areas of mutual dependence and co-operation. A few examples of such important "systems" are organized religion, law enforcement and the judicial process, and education. Those who have been hurt by the failure of one or more of these "systems" to provide their needs or protect them or give them justice will become immune to further admonitions to "trust the system." They will either lose hope or come to new insights about a hope that transcends such human failures.

From the very beginning, the image of the Christian church has suffered because of the sins of omission and commission perpetrated by proponents of the faith, particularly by those in leadership positions. T. V. preachers who are quick to pronounce severe judgments against the sins of others are found to be guilty of those very sins they had denounced as the most distasteful. Reports of sexual abuse by clergy seem to be in the news with increasing regularity. When facing terrible personal crises, church members often receive either no pastoral help from their church community or they are bombarded by mindless (and sometimes condemning) platitudes that try to find meaning in their suffering. If you can't even trust the church, if you can't put your hope in those who are supposed to represent God to you, then whom can you trust?

We depend on a system of law enforcement that will provide reasonable protection on the streets and in our homes. For many, that has broken down. They dare not go outside at night, and hardly in the daytime. Others complain that the police are biased against them and they are constantly targeted and harassed for no good reasons. The jails are full and the courts are clogged with work. Innocent people are sued and obvious offenders are set free because of technicalities and the financial resources to hire a good lawyer. Our hope for justice is tested by failures in the system. If we had assumed that equal justice for all was a reality but now we see that that is not the case, we need to think again about what is the true and lasting basis of hope in a world like ours.

Some have thought that education would be the savior. If everyone has a good education, they will learn how to live together, they will be able to vote intelligently, they will contribute to a healthy economy, and our good society will prosper on into a rosy future. Perhaps we expected too much of our schools. Now days they are asked to be much more than places of learning. They are supposed to be social service centers, a place for hungry kids to get one good meal a day, day care centers for parents who work, a propagator of society's values, and more. And of course the school cannot do all of that. It cannot compensate for what is missing in other areas of our society—especially in the lack of stable and nurturing families and communities.

We are having trouble with many of the "systems" on which society depends for its well-being and attitude of hope. Can these systems be fixed? Surely, we need to concern ourselves with that task. We are called to work and witness within this world and not throw up our hands in despair. But, again, we are reminded that no system is sufficient to lead us to heaven on earth. Some are better than others. All could be improved. The more we can bring God's influence to bear on earthly institutions, the better off we will be. But the world continues to resist that. Jesus tells his disciples, "I have said this to you, so that in me you may have peace. In the world you face persecution. But take courage; I have conquered the world" (John 16:33). In response to Pilate, Jesus says, "My kingdom is not from this world" (John 18:36a).

No human, earthly institutions or systems are perfect. Our final hope is in God, the only one worthy of our deepest hopes, the only one who will never let us down. Even God's church may disappoint and hurt us. But God can still be trusted.

### 4. Not in our health

"He said to her, 'Daughter, your faith has made you well; go in peace, and be healed'" (Mark 5:34).

Many people live their lives as if good health is the most important thing that there is and the continuation of that state of well being is their dominant hope. Sometimes people who have experienced great losses (such as devastation from fire, flood, wind, or theft) will say, "At least we still have our health." On a priority list of things that count the most in our earthly existence, good health is close to the top. Yet, even here we could be in trouble if such an obviously desirable human hope becomes so all consuming that dissapointment in this area leaves one in utter despair. Is there not something (someone) in whom to hope that will still be there even when health fails us?

Our society is growing exceedingly health conscious. Nearly every medium sized strip mall contains a shop selling organically grown food. We are increasingly pre-occupied with what we eat, even though contradictory studies continue to confuse us. What is considered good for us by one research team is declared to be harmful by another. Video stores abound with tapes on which beautiful athletic women demonstrate health enhancing aerobic exercises. You, too, can look like this, and live a lot longer besides. One must be careful walking around the lake to avoid being run over by bicyclists and joggers. If one passes by the local health and fitness club on the way to church, the number of cars in the parking lot is a clear testimony to what is most important and the object of hope for a great number of people.

But few of us ever look as good as those people on the exercise video. No matter how carefully we select the food we eat or how hard we push our bodies in exercise, we will age, sometimes become ill, and not live forever. Even the authors of books on jogging have been known to collapse with a heart attack while carrying out the regimen that is meant to prevent such a happening.

Many have put so much faith in their doctors, setting them on a pedastal, giving them unquestioned authority over their own life and death, that they have been greatly hurt by examples of sloppy medical practice and even incompetence among physicians. It is as if we have forgotten that these medical people are also human beings, capable of bad judgment and limited in their ability to know everything about us and our illness. The disillusionment has become so great that now doctors are blamed (and often sued) for honest human fallibility. They were expected to be like God, and we are hurt and angry because they could not live up to our misplaced hopes.

Religious persons often bring God into their hopes for health. Whether or not they are healthy becomes a way of measuring their favor with God. If they become ill and ask God for healing, God's response (or lack of same) to their urgent plea becomes an indicator of the strength of their faith. They have wandered into the dangerous trap of putting God to the test. Perhaps they have been urged in this direction by well-meaning friends who have reminded them that Jesus was able to heal those who had enough faith to make it happen. If the illness remains, or gets worse, they will be tempted to doubt both themselves and God. Their hope was centered more on their ongoing good health than on the God who <u>can</u> bring healing but, more than that, gives hope even in the midst of suffering, provides a vision that can see beyond our immediate situation, and promises to be with us regardless of the outcome of this particular episode in our life.

Good health is obviously to be desired. It is better to make good decisions about food and exercise than to be indifferent toward what we eat and do with our bodies. God does heal both mind and body, and there are mysterious interconnections between physical, emotional, and spiritual health that we do not even begin to understand. But it is not good health that we worship. Only God is worthy of that.

## 5. Not in wisdom (Job 28:28)

For a long time now, we have lived with an almost unquestioning faith in science. There is no problem so huge that it cannot be solved if we put our best minds into the task. Look at all the wonderful accomplishments that have already come our way through the growing body of human knowledge. Diseases that used to terrify the world and decimate the population are now under control—bubonic plague, smallpox, diphtheria, tuberculosis, infantile paralysis. We have made great strides in fighting heart disease and cancer, though the great breakthrough in those areas has not yet been achieved. And so, as we face the future, we look toward science to make our future safe and more comfortable. Human ingenuity and wisdom will find a way to deal with pollution, depletion of natural resources, and over-population. New methods of transportation and communication will soon make today's wonders obsolete. Diseases that still seem incurable will be conquered. If we just pour enough money into research, AIDS and breast cancer and leukemia will become only memories of hazards that no longer plague our existence. Human wisdom can accomplish great and wonderful things.

Some have come to the conclusion that we do not need God anymore. Or, if there is a God, "God helps those who help themselves." Religion is relegated to the area of superstition. It may be necessary as a crutch for children or old people or the uneducated or those too weak to take matters into their own hands, but better to trust in what humans can do for themselves than to sit around and wait for God (if there is one) to make this a better world. Much to the consternation of their parents, young people go off to college and come home with such ideas as this. With more maturity, they may yet return to a sense of the mystery and spirituality of life and the desire to be in touch with the power behind the universe.

In a somewhat different way, those inside the religious communities also put great confidence in human wisdom, in their ability to formulate and explain with human logic what God thinks and why God is acting in a certain way. They will tell a sufferer why God has brought her suffering. They will interpret a natural disaster as God's punishment for the prevalence of sin in a certain city. They will see a sudden death as an effort by God to teach the survivors something. They claim to know more than a human being can know and to pass their human wisdom off as divine truth.

Others believe that if we study long and hard enough we will be able to understand God in ways that have not yet been achieved. To be sure, there are limitations to human knowledge about God and some mysteries will always remain, but we ought not give in and claim ignorance too soon. We should push ahead and try to know more, even about God, himself. There is a lot of anti-intellectualiam in our church, a feeling that the truth needs to be protected from honest inquiry, a retreat into unassailable pronouncements when seekers come asking their hard questions. God gave humans brains and the ability to think. That is a gift not to be scorned. But what are the limits? How much can we know? When do we decide that this is about as far as we can go using our own powers of wisdom, and we must fall back on the mercy and grace of God in the hope that God will tend to those things that are beyond human comprehension?

Again we face the question of how much to place our hope in what is earthly and human without letting confidence in our own knowledge become a subsitute for hope in the one true God. The 28th chapter of Job is a hymn to wisdom that tries to honor and value human wisdom but admits that true wisdom is known only by God. God established wisdom as part of creation for the benefit of us all, but God tells us that "Truly, the fear of the Lord, that is wisdom; and to depart from evil is understanding" (Job 28:28).

## 6. Not in peace of mind or psychological well-being (John 14:27)

What is the relationship between religion and psychology, between the search for spiritual peace and emotional health, between the work of the parish pastor and the secular counselor? Both religion and psychology want to help people, to give them a sense of integrity and identity and purpose. At least as far as human goals are concerned, they have much in common. Pastoral counselors have been eager to learn from the social scientists and to borrow their theories and techniques. There has not been so much recognition of value and borrowing from the other direction.

Everyone prefers to feel good rather than bad. No one enjoys going through emotional or spiritual turmoil. We seek ways to remove burdens that we carry from unpleasant, even abusive, experiences of childhood. Many of us have difficulties developing intimate relationships, trusting others, making commitments, being assertive without dominating or controlling another. Many of us know that we need help. And there are many out there who are offering to provide that help for us. New gurus arrive on the scene with regularity, selling their self-help books, promising to provide the method that will make our life happy and, perhaps, profitable (if not for us, at least for them).

In the past, many were too embarrassed to admit such needs. To admit to emotional difficulties or to problems in a marital relationship was to confess to weakness and failure. Few wanted to let their pastor or others in their church know about these private areas of their life. Perhaps they would seek help elsewhere, or they would attempt to ride out the storm on their own. Gradually, pastors and other spiritual leaders began to assume the role of counselor. They knew that God did not want people to be miserable and, in addition, sometimes distorted relationships on the human level interfere with one's connection with God. How can a person properly understand God as a father if the only father one has experienced was a violent, unloving, moody, bully who never came home except to beat up on the wife and kids? How can I put my hope in a God who looks like a mean and angry husband? Sometimes we must deal with our perspective on other humans before the images we attribute to God can be helpful rather than confusing or hurtful. So good counseling can be of great value, whether done by those in or outside the church.

But the search for psychological well being is not the same thing as a search for God. Salvation is not the same as emotional health. Preoccupation with my own sense of worth is not to be equated with Christian understanding of self, which recognizes that we are both saint and sinner, of great value but also capable of causing great mischief. The therapist is not the priest and the counselling session is not the liturgy. The support community is not the church.

Sometimes God has a message that is not intended to make us feel good, but, rather, is meant to remind us of our failure to love as we ought and to care for rather than exploit those weaker than we. Though Jesus certainly brought a word of comfort and affirmation to many who felt condemned by their society and their religion, he also spoke words that so infuriated some of his listeners that they plotted to kill him. True religion, though its ultimate message is hopeful, is not only about feeling good.

Further, some people never do "feel good" according to worldly standards. The depression, the schizophrenia, the chemical imbalance, the deep scars of childhood never go away and peace of mind is never a normal state for them. And yet they can have hope. Their persistent unhappiness is not a sign of God's abandonment nor something they will be doomed to endure through eternity. God is present for them also, even if they have not been blessed with the ability to enjoy and be happy in that promise. Jesus said, "Peace I leave with you; my peace I give to you. I do not give to you as the world gives. Do not let your hearts be troubled, and do not let them be afraid" (John 14:27).

### 7. Not in a God we can manipulate or control

"Ask and it will be given you; search and you will find; knock and the door will be opened for you. For everyone who asks receives. ." (Matt. 7:7-8a).

We believe in a God who responds to our need for hope and is attentive to our prayers. But there is a fine, though very important, distinction between a God who interacts with us in a responsive way and a God who does what we tell him to do. The former is promised by Scripture. Adam and Eve are given clothes for the here and now and a hopeful word about the eventual deliverance of the human race. Noah is saved from the flood and receives a promise from God, symbolized by the rainbow, that God will never do that again. Abraham and Sarah believe God's promises and maintain their faith through many obstacles. And so it is with the Israelites in the wilderness, David after his great sin, Habakkuk,

Job, Isaiah, Jeremiah, Paul, and a host of other biblical personalities. God was with them and responded in ways appropriate to their concerns, though not always exactly as they hoped.

God is present. God hears our prayer. God responds. But God is not controlled or manipulated by us. When the Bible emphasizes God's responsiveness, even Gods' willingness to be persuaded and moved by our situation and requests, it is not saying that God will put into action any directive which we send his way. Assuring words that "faith can move mountains" or encouragement to "ask and it will be given to you" are sometimes understood to mean that we can get anything we want from God if we just say it right, with enough sincerity and faith. To believe we have that kind of control is constantly to put our faith on the line. Each specific request becomes a test whether God will prove himself by doing our bidding. We have made our hope in God unnecessarily dependent on the success or failure of a test that we ourselves (not God) have set up.

A few thoughts on the inadequacies and dangers of human overconfidence that we can control God's actions:

(a) Such a belief assumes that we know better than God what should be done. I sometimes think, in times of complaint and worry about what is going on in the world, that if I were God I would do things differently. I would stop the wars and heal the diseases and eliminate poverty and make people love each other. I would not let innocent children be abused or allow young mothers to die of cancer. I would have done something to remove villains like Hitler or Stalin before they had the chance to slaughter millions of people. Sometimes I joke about my list of questions that I want to take up with God when we get the chance to meet face to face in the next life. Such thoughts are, of course, impertinent, even if intended in a playful manner. It would be frightening to think that any human could act as God. Better to live with the mystery of God's activity (or seeming inactivity) than to believe that any mere human knows better than God what is best for the future of the human race and the well-being of God's creation.

(b) In this world, as presently constituted, it is hard to separate what is God's will in a particular event from what is the work of sinful human beings. Life on this planet is a mix of human freedom and God's control. Persons of faith will come to different conclusions as they try to maintain a logical balance between their hope that God is controlling events and their recognition that human beings seem to be free to defy God's will. For whatever reason, God appears to be not yet ready to put an end to human sinful behavior. If, for example, our hope and prayer is that God will intervene to persuade warring parties to cease their conflict, we may be asking more than God is willing to do, at least for now. We cannot control God. In fact, God, himself, seems to have chosen not to manipulate and control us—at least, not completely and not for now.

(c) Our lives are intricately inter-connected with others, within families, neighborhoods, even globally. God could not act to meet each individual's hope without that action having some effect (possibly a negative one) on others. Even if God wanted to be our Genie in the lamp, jumping to fulfill our every wish, it would be impossible to satisy every competing request. You cannot have sunshine for the vacationer and rain for the farmer at the same time. To believe that God is only interested in our own hopes is a very self-centered attitude.

And so we place our hopes in a God who responds to us, who knows us and comes to address our need. But we do not hope in a God whom we can manipulate, who always does whatever we ask. That would be a God too small and unworthy of our hope.

### 8. Only in the God of the Bible

"I am the Lord your God, who brought you out of the land of Egypt, out of the house of slavery; you shall have no other gods before me" (Exod. 20:2-3)

On the human level, there are many systems and institutions that we trust and persons in whom we place our hope—up to a point. We do not wish to be completely cynical, untrusting, and negative about our hopes for this world. People with attitudes like that will drive their families crazy and alienate their friends. Worldly hopes have their place. But none are expansive enough to deal with the total range of human experience, including sin, failure, despair, and death.

And so we hope, ultimately, only in the God that we know from the Bible—the God who created the world and saved the Hebrew slaves from Egypt, who gave the law as a guide and a structure for living together in society, who never forgot his people even during their terrible time in exile, who fulfilled his promises for a new messiah in the coming of Jesus, who loved us so much that he was willing to die for us, who understands our longings and hopes and dreams because he has also lived a human life and experienced suffering and death.

It is in that God, and only that God, that we place our hopes. No other one, no other thing, can provide hope that will last forever. Listen to some of the biblical words of affirmation about the God of our hoping.

"For surely I know the plans I have for you, says the Lord, plans for your welfare and not for harm, to give you a future with hope. Then when you call upon me and come and pray to me, I will hear you. When you search for me, you will find me, if you seek me with all your heart. I will let you find me, says the Lord" (Jer. 29:11-14a).

"Truly the eye of the Lord is on those who fear him, on those who hope in his steadfast love...Let your steadfast love, O Lord, be upon us, even as we hope in you" (Ps. 33:18,22).

In Psalms 42 and 43, the following verse is repeated three times: "Why are you cast down, O my soul, and why are you disquieted within me? Hope in God; for I shall again praise him, my help and my God" (Ps. 42:5 and 11; 43:5).

"For God alone my soul waits in silence, for my hope is from him. He alone is my rock and my salvation, my fortress; I shall not be shaken. On God rests my deliverance and my honor; my mighty rock, my refuge is in God. Trust in him at all times, O people; pour out your heart before him; God is a refuge for us" (Ps. 62:5-8).

The wonderful eighth chapter of Romans ends with these words: "For I am convinced that neither death, nor life, nor angels, nor rulers, nor things present, nor things to come, nor powers, nor height, nor depth, nor anything else in all creation, will be able to separate us from the love of God in Christ Jesus our Lord" (Rom. 8:38-39). If God is for us, nothing can prevail against us. The future is not to be feared, but can be faced with confidence. We have a God who has promised to make that so.

## E. The Transition from Despair to Hope

We all need hope. If all is going well, we hope that our good fortune will continue. If we have fallen on hard times, we hope that things will improve. Sometimes, the suffering is so bad that we lose hope. We cannot imagine a way out of the desperate situation we are in. It is as if we are doomed forever (or at least for the rest of this earthly life) to remain trapped in the pit of pain and suffering. Some of our biblical ancestors found themselves in terrible predicaments, at least as bad as those that we experience. The witness of their struggle to renew hope and the process by which their hope was revived can be instructive for us in our own journeys of faith.

### 1. Hope when there is no hope
"Why did I come forth from the womb to see toil and sorrow, and spend my days in shame?" (Jer. 20:18).

The Bible is more open to the expression of despair, fear, anxiety, and hopelessness than most of us are willing to admit. Many biblical passages are available as a resource to give us permission to be honest and process our negative responses to suffering. But there are a few texts that are unusual because they do not make the effort to move us from despair to hope. They simply allow for the statement of a terrible lament, and then leave it alone. When we read these passages we may ask what such negative material is doing in the Bible, or we may want to fix the message so that it can say more than it actually says. It is hard to leave well enough alone.

Two examples of such material are Ps. 88 and Jer. 20:14-18. Unlike other laments in the book of Psalms, Ps. 88 does not move us from complaint to praise. There is no happy ending. The psalm is filled with painful outbursts directed toward God. God is held responsible for the awful situation of the psalmist with frequent expressions of "<u>You</u> did this or that to me." There is even a little bargaining going on as God is reminded that no one serves or praises God in the grave, and surely God wants people's praise (vv. 10-12). Such expressions are not uncommon in the Psalms but, in this case, the questioning and complaining continue right to the last verse with no sign of change in the heart or mind of the one who is praying. What kind of an example is that for the believer who must endure the trials of life?

Jeremiah had a terrible life, largely because God had called him to preach a dismal prophecy to an unreceptive people. At several places in his book, Jeremiah opens his soul and protests bitterly what God has done to him. A series of personal laments culminates in 20:14-18, where he opens by cursing the day of his birth and closes with the question why he was ever born to spend his days in shame.

What do we do with such negative words? Is there any pastoral use for them? Can they help bring one back to hope or will they only reinforce the hopelessnes that one already feels? A few thoughts on this:

(a) Just saying the painful words can have a helpful effect. On the emotional level, the catharsis of getting it out, putting words to our hurt, can bring some (though perhaps modest) relief. Better to find a way to express and release the stress than to allow it to tear at our insides. And, on the intellectual level, we may be helped by naming our pain, by looking at it and analyzing it and comparing it to the experience of others. Even though we can find no answers, there is often some benefit in ordering our questions.

(b) The value of the unresolved outburst of pain is much greater if we know that someone is listening. The psalmist, clearly, is talking to God. He has not given up on God. He is dealing directly with the one whom he holds responsible for this world and what has happened to him. As long as the conversation continues, there is hope that, sooner or later, God's word of promise will reassert itself and hope will return. Jeremiah may not be addressing God directly, but God is always in his mind as he contemplates his disastrous ministry. So, if we know that God is listening to our desperate words, there is a glimmer of hope present. And also, on the human level, if we can find one who is patient enough to listen and to tough it out with us until hope again appears, there is a good chance that relief will come sooner than if we were forced to pour out our lament in isolation.

(c) These texts with no happy ending remind us of the gift that we can bring to hopeless people by not forcing them to change, by accepting them in their present plight, and by our willingness to give them our presence until things get better. If they are still too deep in trouble to see anything beyond the present, we can give them a slight nudge toward hope by letting them be where they are without, subtly or otherwise, suggesting that they should not think or feel like that. It is hard to resist trying to fix the despairing outlook of a loved one or good friend. But to refrain from doing so may be the most helpful thing we can do and, in the long run, the most likely approach to achieve a renewal of hope.

### 2. From lament to praise

"How long, O Lord? Will you forget me forever? . . But I trusted in your steadfast love; my heart shall rejoice in your salvation. I will sing to the Lord, because he has dealt bountifully with me" (Psalm 13:1a, 5-6).

The most common type of psalm in the book of Psalms is the individual lament. Almost all of these psalms share certain common characteristics. They are prayers, which means they presuppose a God who is listening. They begin with the lament, the complaint, the airing of the problem that God is asked to resolve. At some point, there is a shift, often very sudden, from despair to hope, from lament to praise. Now the psalmist knows that God has heard, relief is coming, and once more it will be possible to come before God with praise rather than a long list of troubles.

Psalm 13 is a classic example of this lament form, with the dramatic shift to hope between verses 4 and 5. The change is a complete turn around. In the space of 6 short verses a despairing person has moved back to trust and hope in God. How does this work? It seems too good to be true. If we could find the formula to help people make that transition, we could be the best counselors in the world and perhaps write a book that would outsell all the self-help offerings on the bookstore shelf. Many have looked at this shift from lament to praise and come to a variety of conclusions. Let us consider a few points.

(a) It is easier to move back to hope once you have had the opportunity to express just how bad things really are. A despairing person will resist words of hope that are spoken prematurely. Hope presented too soon may sound trivial, superficial, almost as if the reality of one's situation is denied or belittled. The complaint, the lament, must come first before we can open the door to the possibility that things will get better. Obviously, our goal is to move ourselves or others out of the need to lament and to recover the ability to praise. But that process, that transition, will not be speeded by cutting short one's need to let the lament run its course.

(b) The flow of the lament structure, from complaint to praise, represents, in a nutshell, the experience of countless persons of faith who have gone before us. They, too, have had their perilous journeys through doubt, fear, anxiety, abandonment, pain, and grief. They, too, have felt that God had left them or punished them unfairly. They, too, have lost all hope that things will get better. And they have offered these terrible thoughts and feelings to God in their prayers. There is no prayer that is unacceptable to God if it is a genuine expression of our own mind and heart. These spiritual ancestors are a model for us of God's willingness to hear the complaint of a troubled person.

But they are also a model of the transition that is possible. People who have been there before, who have endured situations at least as bad as our own, have recovered. They can praise again. Their hope has returned. As we identify ourselves with their pain and suffering, so also we can identify with the move back to confidence in God and hope for the future. Though we cannot control when and how that transition will come, though it will surely take longer than the time required to say the 6 verses of the psalm, the promise of a return to hope is real and is held before us every time we read one of these psalms. God will see that hope returns. It has happened before. It will happen again.

(c) For those who are still trapped in the first part of the psalm, who cannot imagine that hope can ever be a reality for them again, the ending of the psalm may sound simplistic, too neat and tidy. They may need to spend more time in lamenting. Their experience of Good Friday may be so overwhelming that the promise of a resurrection at Easter seems only wishful thinking. Nevertheless, the form of the lament psalm is there for them when they are ready to absorb its message. Others who were as hopeless as they have returned to praise of God. God wants what is good for us and will not let the lament continue forever. We have the testimony to that truth from a multitude of men and women of faith who have seen themselves in the experience of the psalmist.

### 3. Hope when the outcome is in doubt (Lam. 3:19-33)

The book of Lamentations offers a different way to think about moving from despair to hope. There is no happy ending to this book. The outcome is still in doubt. Jerusalem has been destroyed. The ruthless Babylonians have removed the king, slaughtered any resistors, exiled the surviving leaders of the community, and left a remnant of the population to suffer the terrible aftermath of hunger and disease and death. It doesn't get much worse than this. Where is the God who made an everlasting covenant with the house of David and promised to protect the holy city of Jerusalem from all foes? Is God going to do anything to remedy the situation? Have we been deceived by false promises from God? Is our God not as powerful as the God of the Babylonians? Have we so offended God that we will now be cut off forever? Such questions are still there at the end of the book (see Lam. 5:20). The last two verses ask God to restore and renew, but then raise the awful possibility—"unless you have utterly rejected us, and are angry with us beyond measure" (Lam. 5:22). There is no solution, no answer to all the hard questions. The writer does not yet know what will happen. The misery continues and no one can predict how it will end.

But there is hope even in the midst of such terrible suffering, even when we cannot suppress the unthinkable thought that God has abandoned us. Now the words of hope are in the middle of the book, not at the end, because the final outcome is still in doubt. Lam. 3:19-33 contains one of the loveliest expressions of hope anywhere in the Bible. Though misery is all around and there seems to be no relief coming, the writer recalls some of God's attributes that we should constantly keep in mind if hope is to remain. God's steadfast love never ceases and God's mercy is new every morning (vv. 22-24). The Lord is good to those who wait for him (v. 25) and it is good to wait patiently for the salvation that will come (v. 26). "For the Lord will not reject forever. Although he causes grief, he will have compassion according to the abundance of his steadfast love; for he does not willingly afflict or grieve anyone" (Lam. 3:31-33).

Here is a model of hope when one is still too mired in the immediacy of suffering to identify with the generalized process of the lament psalm, the movement down the mountain into despair and up the other side to renewed praise. If there is to be hope when there are no earthly signs of hope, it must come from the middle, from the inside, from the core of one's being. If hope is to survive, it will be built on a return to the basic promises that one has learned about a God who will not leave us even though there is no immediate evidence that relief is coming. If we trust those fundamental statements about a God who is steadfast in love, constant in mercy, and more willing to love and forgive than to punish, then hope is still possible. The questions will remain. The doubts never completely go away. Trouble may continue to swirl around like a wild storm that is out of control. But, at the center, we hang on desperately to our belief in a God who loves us and will find some way out of this mess. That thought is like an anchor to keep us from drifting away into total despair. And so we say with the writer of Lamentations, "But this I call to mind, and therefore I have hope" (Lam. 3:21).

### 4. Job's spiritual journey (Job 42:1-6)

Our friend Job went through several significant transitions in and out of hope. We can benefit from a closer look at the successive stages in his spiritual journey.

At the beginning, Job lived with the hope that his pleasant life would continue long into the future. He believed that by obeying God and turning away from evil, he could increase the probability that he and his family would have a bright future. God will reward the faithful and punish the wicked. Further, proper attention to the rituals provided by his religious community will ensure God's forgiveness for the inadvertent sins of his children (Job 1:5). In short, he believed that he could have some control over his own and his children's destiny. As long as God kept God's end of the bargain, the future looked good.

Then everything went wrong. Job lost everything. He was numb with shock. He tried to hang on to the faith of the past. He continued to utter pious sentiments about how God has the power and authority both to give and take away and he continued to bless the Lord (1:21). Like many who say "It must be God's will" when something horrible happens, Job worked hard to hold on to the conviction that God is all powerful and God knows best. When people who are enduring terrible circumstances still speak boldly about the goodness of God, they may be saying more (or less) than first seems apparent. Such pious expressions could, in fact, be sincere statements of trust in God. They could also indicate a compulsion to say something religious, the need to articulate some word about God even if we don't know what to say. Or they could be an attempt to hide one's growing anger toward a God who would permit such catastrophes. Whatever Job meant, it soon became clear that it was too soon for him to move directly to renewed hope. The process would be much more painful and take much longer than Job expected or wanted. Job had tried to reach a state of peace and comfort by assuring himself of God's providence but, unfortunately, he was in too much agony for that to happen yet.

The next stage in Job's journey was a long period of lamenting and questioning. It began with his cursing of the day of his birth (3:1). From there he proceeded to argue fiercely with his friends about their interpretation of his calamities, to express doubts that God was just, to reminisce about the good old days when he and God were friends, and to ask God either to leave him alone or to let him know what great wrong he had done that he should be punished so severely. This is the part of Job's spiritual pilgrimage that we often neglect as we choose to remember only the "patience" of Job.

Finally, Job has an encounter with God. It is not at all what he had imagined. He has no opportunity to make the case that he is a good, undeserving person and the victim of a miscarriage of justice. God overwhelms him with talk of the wonders of creation and the inability of human beings (like Job) to make and provide for the created world. There are some things that only God can know and do. Job is still not given an explanation for his suffering. He had come with his list of intellectual questions, his desire to know "why," but what he received was a relational answer.

And so Job found it possible to move on to another stage in his spiritual travels in and out of hope. Something happened to him in his direct encounter with God. Failure to hear precise reasons for his suffering did not prevent him from returning to trust in God. God had heard him. God had spoken. God cared about him and persisted in seeking him out, not satisfied to leave him in his tormented state. Job was again reminded of human limitations and the need to trust God for what we can neither understand nor control. Job may have known that in his mind, but now he knew it in his heart and soul. And he could live with it. God could again be trusted, and where there is trust there is hope. Job says to God, "I had heard of you by the hearing of the ear, but now my eye sees you" (Job 42:5).

[margin note: Yes]

And so Job, at the end, comes to the place where he wanted to be when the disasters first struck. But at that time his brave efforts to hang on to hope were not sufficient to deal with the terrible losses that he had endured. Before returning to uncomplicated trust in God, he had to go through a long wilderness of pain and doubt and anger and distrust. Even then, in those bitter days, God was with him, looking for an opening, trying to communicate a word of grace. Though Job was not always aware of it, God had never let go of him. Finally, Job heard, trusted again, and lived the rest of his life in hope.

### 5. Suffering produces hope (Rom. 5:1-5)

At the beginning of Romans 5, Paul tells his readers that, since they are justified by faith and can be assured of God's grace, they should "rejoice" in their suffering (some translations say "boast"—Rom. 5:3). That has always struck me as curious advice. It sounds morbid, even masochistic, that one should enjoy and glory in something as unpleasant as suffering. Perhaps this word of advice has even played a part in suppressing our human need to lament during terrible ordeals. If Christians are expected to rejoice when their life takes a hellish turn, then how can they admit to thoughts and feelings of betrayal, bitterness, doubt, and anger? Paul seems to turn normal human responses to suffering upside down. He says that, as bad as it seems, suffering can be a good thing with benefits for the sufferer. It can produce hope rather than destroy hope. At first glance, this seems like wishful thinking, as if we can make the transition from despair to hope just by forcing ourselves to rejoice— even when there is no joy. I am always offended when I hear that someone has admonished the sufferer of a terrible loss to "Praise God anyway."

Over the years, I have come to appreciate this text more and more, even as I recognize that for some it sounds like a condemnation of their inability to rejoice when there seems no good reason to do so. Suffering can produce hope, but there are some qualifications in Paul's endorsement of this possibility.

(a) The passage in Romans 5 begins with the affirmation that we are saved by our faith in God's grace. That gives us peace in the knowledge that we have access to a God who is merciful (Rom. 5:1-2). If suffering is ever to produce good results and even lead to renewed hope, it helps if one starts with the conviction that God loves unconditionally, takes no delight in punishing, and has already decided that we are in his favor. Knowing that, we will be less tempted to interpret our suffering as punishment or indifference or arbitrariness on God's part. The move from suffering to hope will not come easily for those without this basic trusting relationship with God.

(b) Like the writer of the lament psalm, Paul is speaking after the fact, from his own personal experience. He is not theorizing in the abstract, only imagining what might be possible. In some strange way, his suffering has made him closer to God than he was before. His hope has been strengthened and now rests on a surer foundation because he has suffered. Many Christians throughout the ages have agreed with Paul and have left us testimony of their spiritual growth as a result of their suffering. This may not be the experience of everyone, but there is no doubt that it has worked for many, including the great St. Paul, himself.

(c) Suffering has a way of knocking down our false hopes. Maybe we have put our trust for a bright future in human authorities, material possessions, physical health, institutions of government and church. But then events in our life make it clear that if this is all there is, it isn't enough. When all the human props are gone and only suffering remains, where does one go to find hope? That was a question that confronted Paul. He found that everything in which he had previously placed his hopes was inadequate to the task. And the process of coming to that conclusion was very painful. Paul could not be let down, disappointed, or disillusioned any further. Even life, itself, could be taken from him at any time by hostile authorities. The worst that the world could bring had already happened. What now? To be sure, the inadequacy of false and partial hopes had been revealed to Paul. But, is that good news or bad news? His suffering had succeeded in showing him that, but was there now any place else to turn?

(d) When all human hope has dissolved in the face of relentless suffering, God is there. At that most terrible time when all has been lost, the one who loved us enough to die for us is present. And, therefore, hope is possible. If God had not been there, the journey downward into suffering would have ended in despair. But when one enters that lowest of times, when all defenses are down, when (as a last resort, perhaps) there is no where else to turn but to God, God is there. And the God who is present is the same God whom Paul describes at the beginning of this passage, full of grace and love and compassion. Now, having hit the bottom, one is no longer distracted by false hopes. The only one who is still there is the true God who will never abandon us no matter what our experience in a world of less than permanent hope. Suffering, indeed, has produced hope, "and hope does not disappoint us" (Rom. 5:5a).

## F. Hope Beyond the Present World

If all our hopes are to be achieved, we must have more time. If God is going to accomplish all that has been promised—peace, justice, prosperity, health, happiness, relationships of reconciliation and love—then we certainly need more time than the short lifespan of even the most aged among us. And, since the world continues as a battleground where sin and evil win many of the battles, just having more time may not be enough. Until there is a radically new world, much different from the one we know, our hopes will remain partial and incomplete. Christians have speculated for centuries whether that new age will begin with a tumultuous end time when everything changes in the twinkling of an eye and the dead are raised for reward or punishment, or as a more private transition when each individual walks through the door of death to a new life with God in heaven.

The Bible speaks in many ways to our need for more time and/or a new age if our hopes are to be completed. There is a development as we move through Scripture from beginning to end. Early Old Testament passages have few expressions of hope for an individual life that extends beyond the grave. This hope is more clearly articulated in late Old Testament and in the New Testament.

### 1. Community in life and death (Gen. 49:29-50:3)

The story of the death of Jacob presents a view of death that is common throughout much of the Old Testament. There is no talk here of a resurrection, no promise that Jacob will return to life on earth, no expression of hope that his spirit will move into a new and more wonderful existence in which all the problems of this life are removed. Nevertheless, in its references to community among both the deceased and the living, this passage provides some valuable insights.

Apparently, those who left us the stories and sayings and poetry and songs of the old Testament did not feel the need to work out the details of what happens to people when they die. That was a mystery that they could not solve and they did not feel the compulsion to try. They had such a strong sense of community, of identification with their people who had lived before and who would come later, that they could imagine themselves living on in the lives of their descendants. They knew that God was faithful and would still be in relationship with their people, even if they were not alive to see it. Their long-term hopes were for the improvement of this world, not for a heaven for themselves. What God and humans were not able to accomplish during the lifetime of an individual could still happen when the time was right. It is hard for most of us, after centuries of western individualism, to appreciate fully the meaning and comfort conveyed by such a sense of corporateness, of oneness with others. To recover that, even in some small way, might help alleviate our fear of death, our terror that we will be obliterated as individuals.

The writer of this story describes death as "to be gathered to one's people" (Gen. 49:29,33). There is community among the dead, whatever else one might conjecture about what awaits us after death. This hope is symbolized by Jacob's insistence that he be buried in the family burial plot, next to his wife Leah and with his parents and grandparents (Gen. 49:29-32). There is continuity between the living and the dead and there is community among the dead. It is important where one is buried. When we wander through the burial plot in our hometown we are reminded who we are, where we came from, what has shaped us and made us. To read on the tombstones the names and dates of birth and death is to reconstruct the family history. And as we read and meditate on those ancestors who went before, they live on in our memory in a kind of immortality. One of the tragedies in our urban, mobile society is the lack of such places where we can connect with the past and think about our future. Most people do not want to think about where they will be buried. They resist when the local cemetery calls on the phone and tries to sell them a burial plot complete with perpetual care. Many do not know where they will be living next year or next decade, let alone where they, or their children, will be when they die.

When Jacob dies, he leaves behind a community of the living who then mourn the loss of one whom they loved. There are things that they can do, together, as a community, to ease the grief of

Jacob's passing. Joseph weeps and kisses his father good-bye (Gen. 50:1). Then the embalmers and the mourners go to work, with prescribed rituals, to help the community deal with this particular death (Gen. 50:2-3). Life goes on. But, before the resumption of normal life, time is set aside to grieve for oneself and to honor the deceased. All our communities have developed specific rituals to help us deal with grief and loss. Some of them are more helpful than others. It is of great importance that a supportive community do them together.

In Jacob's day, hope for life after death was not spelled out in detail. We must look elsewhere in the Bible for that. But even in this story, we can find hope in the emphasis on community. The one who has died is still in a community, with family and with God. And those of us who are left behind need supportive communities to lead us through dark times of grief so that we can resume a life that is lived in hope.

### 2. Job almost believes (Job 14:7-19)

Many people find it hard to believe in the possibility that they will live again after they die. They would like to believe. They know in their heart that this world cannot be all that there is. But it seems almost too good to be true. The skepticism of a scientific age, which wants visible proof before acceptance of any proposition as true, has only added to the difficulty of hanging on to specific hopes that go beyond human ability to verify them. Those of us who want to believe but find it difficult to do so can understand the struggle of Job as he thinks about the likelihood for life after death in Job 14.

In most of his conversations with his friends and with God, Job laments that there is no life after death. The innocent and the wicked all end up together in the ground without any distinctions. There is no reward for those who have suffered unfairly and no punishment for those who have made themselves rich through their abuse of others. His lack of hope for an afterlife in which justice will finally be done adds greatly to the pain of his own suffering.

But in chapter 14, Job opens up the possibility that maybe, just maybe, there could be more to our existence than we can see from this side of the grave. He looks at a tree and that starts him thinking. If a tree that is cut down, leaving nothing but a dead looking stump, can bring forth new growth at the scent of water, why shouldn't the same be possible for humans (Job 14:7-12)? The miracle of the rebirth of nature, when the warm sun of spring melts the snow and ice or the first autumn rains turn the brown hillside into a glorious green, has long served as a reminder and example of God's power to bring life from death. At least in the northern hemisphere, where Easter coincides with the wondrous awakening of spring, Easter sermons often refer to the rebirth of nature as a sign of God's intention to revive what had seemed to be forever lifeless.

In 14:14, Job asks the key question, "If mortals die, will they live again?" If only that were true. If only he could be assured that his present experience was not the end of the story. God has come to be an enemy who has caused his trouble, who seems angry and vindictive for no good reason, who will not answer Job's questions about why he should be suffering. If only God would let him sleep quietly in Sheol until things have cooled down, until God's anger has subsided (14:13). Then, God could call for him and Job would answer (14:15). God would no longer keep a book on Job's misdeeds, as if God wants to find something to punish (v. 16). Rather, Job's "transgression would be sealed up in a bag and you (God) would cover over my iniquity" (14:17). If only that were true. If only Job could be sure of that. Then he could have hope again even if his terrible trials continued for a time—even a lifetime. Job almost believes.

But Job's mind won't stop. He can't let it rest. It is still too good to be true. Like water that, if given enough time, will wash away mountains and move the beach further inland, his suffering continues to wear away the fragile hope to which he clings. He has seen the promise of a life forever with a God who loves and forgives. He stands at the door and looks in and thinks how lovely it would be to live there, but he cannot quite bring himself to step inside. And he says to God, "so you destroy the hope of mortals" (14:19b).

Many people in our day are much like Job. "If only it were true. If only I could be sure. Then I could have hope." Many of us believe, but not quite. We are like the man who once told Jesus, "I believe, help thou my unbelief." We need to remember that this is not the end of the story of Job. God will not leave him in this state of indecisiveness. We cannot be sure what Job finally came to believe about his own immortality, but we do know that he again was able to trust God and to leave the mystery of what follows our death in God's hands. If we see ourselves in Job's struggle to believe, let us also take comfort in the assurances that he received through his encounter with God.

### 3. Dry bones will live again

Ezekiel 37:1-14 presents a powerful image. Many are familiar with this picture from the Negro spiritual that captures the mood of renewed hope through the music as well as the words. The prophet is led by the Lord to a valley that is littered with dry bones. They are piled up as far as you can see and they are getting drier and drier as the hot sun bakes them into a white chalk-like substance. It is hard to believe that these bones once had flesh and blood and skin and breath. The bones are the only thing that remains—the rest has been eaten by wild creatures or has deteriorated into dust— to remind us that these were once living and breathing persons. God shows the valley of dry bones to Ezekiel in order to teach him that there is hope even in such a place as this. And then God directs Ezekiel to act, to prophesy, to tell those who have given up hope that God can and will revive even what is as dead as these bones.

A few important points to remember from Ezekiel 37.

(a) This is a word of hope both for this world and the next. Even though we rest our ultimate hope in a God who is present when earthly expectations fail us and there is nothing left but our own death, we should not abandon the confidence that God also works in the here and now. God does answer prayers for things of this world. Sometimes the miracle occurs. God does influence world events and works within the experiences of individual lives. In verses 12-14, God promises to lead the people of Israel out of exile back to their own land. Though the nation has long been destroyed and has been drying up, as these bones, scattered all over the ancient world, God can still put it back together and give it new life. This is a very real and historical hope.

But, in this same passage, Ezekiel speaks about the opening of graves and bringing people up from their graves. We can understand this not only as the revival of the nation of Israel but also as the promise of life after death for individuals. We cannot be sure whether Ezekiel understood it this way but there is no question that the words carry a power, a promise, both for renewal of life within this world and for life after death. Generations of believers have read Ezekiel and have seen hope for their own resurrection in his words.

(b) No dead is too dead for God. God can revive bones that have been disconnected and dried in the hot sun for generations, centuries, millennia. When God asks Ezekiel if these bones can live, Ezekiel replies, "O Lord God, you know" (37:3). Not a bad answer. Perhaps God was testing him a bit to see how he would reply. He has enough faith not to say, "I don't think so, God. I mean, they have been dead for a long, long time. There's no chance." Nor does he jump to the other extreme and blurt out with confidence, "Sure, God. Why not? You can do anything." He throws the question back to God. Ezekiel really doesn't know if it is possible. But, if it can happen, it is only because God has decided to do it. Ezekiel does not know what God intends to do. So he waits for God to let him know. The answer comes immediately. "Yes." God will cause breath to enter the bones, and they will live (37:5).

(c) The word of promise must be spoken to the hopeless so that they can hear and believe and have hope. God tells Ezekiel to prophesy to the bones (37:4, 12), let them know that as hopeless as their situation may seem to be, God can and will bring them back to life. For a time they may remain scattered over the landscape, dry and separate from other bones, without flesh and lifeless. Ezekiel needs to tell the bones (who are, in fact, the hopeless people) what is to come so that they can live in hope until the time when the promise becomes reality. And so, like Ezekiel, we are to hold before the hopeless and lifeless people of this world the vision of a God who can bring us back to life, both individually and collectively, both within this world and the next.

### 4. The Lord will swallow up death forever (Isa. 25:6-9; 26:16-19)

Chapters 24-27 of Isaiah are sometimes called the "Isaiah Apocalypse" because they share some of the characteristics of a particular type of biblical literature. Our best examples of apocalyptic literature in the Bible are in the books of Daniel and Revelation, but we also see examples elsewhere. This kind of material is pessimistic about the state of the world and believes that nothing will improve until God takes direct action to intervene. The present is understood to be a time of great turmoil as the final battle between good and evil approaches. Believers can look forward to relief (though things may get worse for awhile before they get better) when God finally acts to remove all our enemies (sin, suffering, satanic powers, evil) once and for all.

Two passages (Isa. 25:6-9; 26:16-19) present powerful words of hope that the present suffering will not last much longer and all our enemies (including the greatest threat of all—death) will be defeated forever. Looking at these two texts together, we can draw some conclusions about our hope for this final victory.

(a) It has been a long wait. We are reminded of Psalm 13—"How long, O Lord?" To a sufferer, even one more minute of torment is too long. And for some, the minutes pass into hours and days and months and years. "Why doesn't God do something?" Isa. 26:16-18 likens the wait for God to bring relief to a pregnant woman whose labor pains go on and on and on. But she cannot deliver. Instead of a child coming forth, there is only wind. "We have won no victories on earth, and no one is born to inhabit the world" (Isa. 26:18b). The hard time of waiting has been acknowledged. No one doubts the reality of how difficult it has been. But that time is almost over. The end is in sight. And it will be a wonderful time indeed.

(b) The joys of the new age will be like a great feast of rich food and fine wine (Isa. 25:6). It will be the long expected meal envisioned in the liturgy of the Lord's Supper where we eat the bread and drink the cup as "a foretaste of the feast to come." It will be the best dinner party one could ever imagine, filled with joy and celebration and companionship and good feeling. Picture in your mind the most wonderful meal you have ever had, the best party you have ever attended, the tastiest food and friendliest people and most stimulating conversation and prettiest background music. It will be like that. And much, much more.

(c) All that makes us sad, unhappy, fearful, or anxious will be gone forever. God will destroy the shroud that is cast over all people (Isa. 25:7). God will wipe away all tears (25:8). There will no longer be any reason to weep. Everything that has brought us disgrace, shame, embarrassment will be taken away. All this is true. The Lord has spoken (25:8). We have waited long for this. But we waited in the Lord, the one who could be trusted. God has come through as we hoped. And now we will rejoice and be glad in the salvation that God has brought (25:9).

(d) Even death has been defeated. The Lord "will swallow up death forever" (Isa. 25:7). In the mortal combat between good and evil, between God and Satan, between Jesus and the evil powers of the universe, good has devoured evil. For Christians, the Easter story adds another dimension to this Isaiah text. God is victorious. The battle is won. What remains is a mopping up procedure which may still seem dangerous and frightening to us, but the outcome is no longer in doubt. God tells us, through the prophet, "Your dead shall live, their corpses shall rise. O dwellers in the dust, awake and sing for joy! For your dew is a radiant dew" (Isa. 26:19). If even death no longer has the power to claim us, what is there to fear? There should be no more inhibitions to our hope.

### 5. Resurrection followed by judgment

Daniel 12:1-2 contains the clearest statement about the resurrection of the dead anywhere in the Old Testament. Such a hope was implied in earlier biblical passages and many Jews and Christians came to understand them that way (as, for example, the vision of dry bones in Ezekiel). But Daniel states it directly. After a time of the greatest anguish since history began, the people whose name is found written in the book will be delivered (12:1). "Many of those who sleep in the dust of the earth shall awake, some to everlasting life, and some to shame and everlasting contempt" (12:2).

At the time of the writing of Daniel, many had been persecuted and even killed for remaining loyal to their God. The wicked were in power and they were vicious in their suppression of any insubordination. Why should humans stand up against hopeless odds to make a witness for truth if it will cause their death? If this life is all there is, why should one willingly give it up? If God is a God of justice there must be a judgment following this life when innocent martyrs can be rewarded and the perpetrators of evil can be punished. The Hitlers of the world cannot go quietly into oblivion without having to answer for what they have done.

And so Daniel promises a resurrection so that distinctions can be made. Death is not the great equalizer where good and bad, rich and poor, peasant and king, have all arrived at the same status of endless sleep, never to be disturbed again. We are not all the same in death, just as we were not all the same in life. But, there is an important difference. True justice will reign <u>after</u> the resurrection. Often the tables will be turned. Those who had everything in this life may lose it in the next. They may even be punished. Those who were victims, abused and exploited by the powerful, will be rewarded for their faithfulness in the life to come.

Is this good news or bad news? Is this an important word of hope for us or is it something else to worry about as we face not only our future on earth but what lies beyond?

It is good news for those who have suffered for the faith, who have had miserable lives filled with one trial after another. Even persons who have suffered innocently for a lifetime and die in agony can have hope. God is a God of justice who will make sure that good will triumph over evil. Of course, we would like justice to occur while we are alive to see it, but it is not absolutely necessary. God will right the wrongs that have come to us and to others. There is always time for that to happen.

But it is bad news for those who have been disobedient or unfaithful to God and think they have gotten away with it. No matter that they live happy and healthy into a ripe old age and die in peace with their family around the bed and are given a royal send-off by throngs of admirers at a wonderful funeral. God will exact justice from them if their name is not written in the book (Dan. 12:1). We may hear this as good news if we are sure that the negative judgment is intended for someone else, our enemies, people we don't like anyway. But what if we start to question our own status with God? What if we are terribly sensitive about the wrongs that we do, even in very subtle ways that the world would excuse but make us feel guilty? What if we join St. Paul and Martin Luther in our conviction that no human being is good enough to avoid a negative judgment from God? What if our name is not on the list? If we are going to be raised from the dead only to face everlasting contempt (Dan. 12:2), it would surely be better to sleep forever in an undisturbed and unconscious slumber.

If there is a resurrection followed by a judgment, we need assurance that the God who decides about us is loving, forgiving, compassionate. This can be good news and a great source of hope only if we know that we can safely pass the close scrutiny of judgment day. Christians believe that this is possible, not because we are good enough or clever enough but because Jesus Christ has taken care of any necessity for precise justice and is willing to vouch for us. We trust in God's grace and therefore we are justified. Resurrection and judgment are not to be feared. They are, in fact, vital to the hope that sustains us even beyond life itself.

### 6. Promise and warning from Jesus (Luke 16:19-31)

Is there an after life? If there is, what will it be like? We are all curious about this. We search the words of Jesus trying to find some answers to these questions. His teachings carry special authority for us. What clues does he give about what to expect on the other side of death? His parable of the rich man and poor man Lazarus (Luke 16:19-31) provides some interesting thoughts (both troubling and comforting) for us to contemplate as we stretch our minds to envision the mysteries that lie beyond the grave. There is a word of hope in Jesus' story about these two men, their circumstances while still alive, and their situation after death. But, mingled with the hope (as in the message from Daniel 12), there is also a warning. What does Jesus say?

(a) There is no excuse for uncaring, indifferent, contemptuous, undignified treatment of our fellow human beings. As Jesus said in other places, he did not come to remove any of the law. God's commands that we should love one another, treat each other with generosity, and, particularly, be concerned for the weak and vulnerable (such as widows, orphans, sojourners, the hungry and the homeless) are still in place.

(b) There will be rewards for some and punishment for others. That is, the next life will not be the same for all. Not everyone will get a free pass to heaven. Judgments will be made. For Lazarus, it will be a time of comfort, symbolized by the image of resting in Abraham's bosom ("on his lap" or "by his side" according to some translations). For the rich man, it will be a place of endless torment, with heat and flame and no one to bring relief. This parable has contributed to the common picture of hell as a place of fire. The rich man got his reward while still alive. Now he will pay the price for his attitude toward Lazarus. The poor man suffered in this life, but justice will come to him after he dies. The roles have been reversed. There is an undertone of surprise in the response of the rich man to his predicament. He didn't expect it to be like this. If only he had known. It would be terrible if his brothers ended up here also.

(c) People cannot move back and forth between heaven and hell. Their destination has been determined by what they did on earth and now they are stuck with the consequences. The rich man dares to suggest that Abraham should send Lazarus on down to help cool him off. But he is advised that the chasm between these two places cannot be crossed from either direction.

(d) Too many people are obstinate in their refusal to believe that this could happen. They think God does not care, that God has not noticed what they have done with their lives. The rich man asks Abraham to send Lazarus back to life with a warning to his brothers. Abraham responds that human beings already have as much warning as they need. They have Moses and the prophets. Maybe they should go back and read them again. They probably wouldn't pay attention even if one came back from the dead to preach to them (and the irony is that Jesus, in fact, did that and many still have not believed).

There are hard words from Jesus in this parable. We rejoice in the promise of life after death, the opportunity to continue as ourselves into eternity, the necessary time to right all wrongs, the comfort of living forever in close proximity with God and in community with all the saints (even Abraham). But with that promise also comes the fear that we may end up like that rich man, who enjoyed his luxury but was blind to the torment of his neighbor. We are thankful that God is a God of justice. But we also need to be reminded of God's mercy and forgiveness. This particular parable of Jesus is a little heavy on the side of warning. Our hope for a merciful God needs to be reinforced from other biblical words in order to prevent us from undue preoccupation with and fear of God's punishment.

### 7. Today with me in Paradise (Luke 23:39-43)

It was a word of pure grace spoken by Jesus to the man hanging next to him. There were two of them, both criminals. They, like Jesus, were enduring the slow death of execution by crucifixion. One of them screamed at Jesus, perhaps in a sarcastic way, that if Jesus was really the Messiah he should save both himself and them. The other man rebuked the first. They deserved what was happening to them but Jesus had done no wrong. Then, addressing Jesus by name, he said, "Remember me when you come into your kingdom" (Luke 23:42). Jesus replied, "Truly I tell you, today you will be with me in Paradise" (Luke 23:43). What a wonderful word of promise. Nothing else was required. The criminal's confession of responsibility for his own actions and his confidence in Jesus were enough.

Let us think about Jesus' words, dividing them into three parts: today, with me, in Paradise.

"Today." Not tomorrow or next week or next year or 1,000 years from now. Relief is coming today. The pain of dying on a cross must have been awful. But it won't last much longer. It will be gone before this day has past. Hang on a little longer in the knowledge that your time of deliverance is close at hand.

Most biblical passages about life after death refer to a resurrection of the dead at some great climactic endtime, when all those who have died will be brought back to life. This passage is different. It talks about "today." There will not be a long wait. For those who are still alive it may seem like a long wait for God's final defeat of all enemies, for Jesus to come again, for the messes of the world to be cleaned up. But for the one who dies in the Lord, the transition from torment to Paradise, from the pains of this life to the joys of heaven, will seem to be immediate. There will be no wait, no consciousness of separation from God, no sense of isolation while lying asleep in a cold grave. It will all happen today.

"With me." Whatever else we may imagine heaven to be, it will be a place where we are in direct communion with Jesus, with God. All the obstacles that prevent humans from the fullest relationship with the divine will be removed once and for all. No more limitations of sight and sense, no more guilt over real and imagined sins, no more fear of what is to come, no more looking through a glass darkly as we peer ahead into the unknown. The intimacy between creator and creature that was a short-lived reality at the beginning in the garden will be resumed. Jesus has promised. "Today you will be with me in Paradise."

"In Paradise." Paradise is a wonderful word. It conjures up the most beautiful scenes. Each of us can paint our own picture, filling in the details with the most wonderful, comforting, pleasant, happy, and loving images that we can create. Paradise is the best that we can conceive from our human perspective, and then much more. It is, most of all, a relationship with God that will never be broken again, a return to where we belong, to the place where God has always wanted us to be. Jesus promised the criminal dying next to him that they would both be there. We, no less than he, have received the same promise. Thanks be to God.

## 8. Jesus speaks about eternal life in John's Gospel
## (John 3:16; 11:1-44; 14:1-3)

The Gospel of John has preserved for us some of the most beautiful and comforting of all Jesus' promises about hope for life after death. These are very familiar passages to the preacher who searches the words of Jesus for comfort and hope when preparing a funeral sermon.

(a) "For God so loved the world"

My father believed that John 3:16 was the heart of the gospel, the good news in a nutshell. If you have this verse right, if you believe it with all your heart and mind and soul, there really isn't much else to worry about. You might say that everything else in the Bible, every creed or doctrinal statement, every hymn or devotional meditation, is merely commentary on the truth contained in these beautiful words. It gets to the heart of God's motivation, why God sent his son into the world, what God hoped to accomplish through all of this.

It was done out of love. God loves us. That is all the explanation that we need. The God who created the world, who interacts with humanity in ways that are not always clear to us, who allows evil to persist and sometimes seems to bring punishment, is first and foremost a God of love. That is the bottom line. If we want a one word definition of God, "love" is about as good a word as we can find. Everything else needs to be interpreted in light of that basic affirmation. God did not send the Son into the world to condemn it, but to save it (3:17). Surely we can put our future, even what lies in store for us after death, in the hands of a God like this.

(b) "I am the resurrection and the life"

The eleventh chapter of John tells the wonderful story of the raising of Lazarus from the dead by his good friend Jesus. To be sure, Lazarus does not yet enter eternal life. Rather, he is brought back to live some more years in this world. He will have to face another more permanent death later. But the dramatic picture of Lazarus, already dead and presumably rotting after 4 days in the tomb, walking out of his grave at Jesus' command gave a vivid setting for Jesus to make some extraordinary claims about himself.

He even has power over death. If he commands a corpse to get up and walk, it will do so.

Martha had expressed to Jesus her confidence that her brother would rise again at the last days (11:24), but Jesus assures her that power over death is already present in himself. There is no need to wait. When Jesus is with us, death has already been defeated. He says, "I am the resurrection and the life. Those who believe in me, even though they die, will live, and everyone who lives and believes in me will never die" (John 11:25-26).

(c) "Do not let your hearts be troubled"

Jesus reassures his disciples. Stop worrying. Do not be anxious. Do not fear what lies ahead either in this life or beyond. This is easy advice to give, but if one is truly afraid, it is not necessarily easy advice to follow. But Jesus goes on to give some reasons why they should not be afraid. There will be a place for them in his Father's house. I always liked the translation of John 14:2 which I learned as a little boy: "In my father's house are many mansions." Heaven was a place full of mansions, like the part of town where the rich people lived. That picture of stately homes on a wide boulevard with lots of big trees and beautiful flowers was surely part of my first efforts to try to imagine what heaven must be like. Though Jesus has to go away for awhile, they must not interpret that as abandonment. He is going to prepare a place for them.

Then he says, "I will come again and take you to myself, so that where I am there you may be also" (John 14:3). Jesus will return. What we sometimes perceive as the absence of God is only temporary. Jesus' intention is to draw us to himself, to make sure that we will be with him forever. Whatever that means, however we picture it in our minds, whatever images our limited human imagination can create to describe the indescribable, it will be good. We will be with the God who loves us on into eternity. That is enough to know.

### 9. Paul's indifference toward death (Philip. 1:12-26)

Paul is in prison when he writes a letter of encouragement to the Philippians. He is in a precarious position. It is conceivable that his captors will free him so that he can continue his ministry.

Then again, he may be kept in prison for an extended period of time. There is also a strong possibility that he will be put to death. He does not know exactly what the future holds for him but, from a human perspective, it doesn't look very good. He knows that his friends in Philippi are worried about him. So he writes with the intention of supporting them. His words remain as a blessing for all of us latter day believers.

Paul begins by putting a positive construction on what has happened to him. Even his imprisonment has had some benefits for the spread of the gospel. The good news about Jesus Christ has now become known throughout the whole imperial guard (Philip. 1:12-13). What better way to preach to the jail keepers than to be in jail? Paul sees Christ's hand, God's purpose, in what looks to others like a terrible catastrophe for him and the cause of his ministry.

Paul's main hope is not for his own safety, his release from prison, or even avoidance of death. Rather, his primary concern is that he will not be put to shame, that he will not weaken or in any way disgrace the message of Christ. His hope is that Christ will continue to be exalted by his speaking, by the way he lives and, if necessary, by the way that he dies (1:20). Whether or not Christ is glorified is more important to him than his own life. He has put his own personal living or dying in a much larger perspective so that it is no longer what matters most to him.

He then begins to debate in a rather detached analytical way whether it would be better to live or to die. It is Paul's version of Hamlet's "To be or not to be" speech. For Hamlet either possibility was negative. With Paul, both options are good ones. There is a case to be made for dying so that one can be with Christ. If Paul had his choice, he might be inclined to take that one (Philip. 1:23). Human limitations make a complete relationship with Christ impossible. That can come only after death. But there is also a strong argument for staying alive, for carrying on fruitful labor, for teaching and encouraging the struggling churches that still depend on Paul's wisdom (1:22, 24-26).

There is no fear of death here. Nor is there a desire to flee from life. This is not a morbid fascination with death, surely not a contemplation of suicide. What we see in Paul is an amazing indifference toward life or death. He is so confident in his relationship with God through Christ that whatever comes will be all right. If God has more for him to do, he is willing and eager to carry on. If his earthly mission is over, that could be even better. Let God decide. Paul would have a hard time choosing if the choice were left to him. "For to me, living is Christ and dying is gain" (1:21). Oh to have the faith of Paul, to thumb our nose at death and say, "You don't scare me. I am with Christ, dead or alive, now and forever. There is nothing you can do to hurt me."

### 10. What is a "spiritual body?" (1 Cor. 15)

In this important chapter, Paul reflects on what we will be like after the last trumpet sounds and the dead are resurrected into a new and different kind of existence. Paul anticipates some of the questions that he knows are floating around out there among those first Christians (v. 35). In every age, especially when confronting death in themselvs or in loved ones, people have come to their pastors and asked for some thoughts about what heaven will be like. In this great chapter, Paul tries to say something that makes sense, is consistent with what he knows about God, is informed by his faith in Christ, and allows for some human speculation about the mystery.

Early in the chapter, Paul makes it clear what is the center of the gospel message for him: Christ died for our sins, was buried, rose on the third day, and appeared to many people, lastly to Paul, himself (1 Cor. 15:3-8). Christ's resurrection and the resurrection of the dead are very closely inter-twined in Paul's reasoning. If one is not true, neither is the other. To doubt the resurrection of the dead is to doubt that Jesus rose from the dead. And vice versa. You can't have one without the other (15:12-19).

Granted all this, assuming we believe that a resurrection is possible, what will we be like? Paul forges ahead in an attempt to speak about what we have not yet seen, to sneak a look at what exists beyond the grave or after the endtime.

We will have a body. We will not be a free spirit floating around, a wisp of smoke, a piece of cloud, a gentle breeze. We will be substantial, recognizable, clearly identifiable as the persons that we are. But we will be different. It could not be heaven if it was merely more of the same—acne, the common cold, aches in the joints when the weather changes, stomach upset and sunburn. What we have now are physical bodies. But in the new age, when the end comes, when the dead rise and all of us change, we will have "spiritual bodies." In order to describe these mysteries, Paul has chosen to join together two words which are normally considered to be opposites—spiritual and body.

Paul fills out what he means by this by contrasting characteristics of the old (present) physical body with those of the new (after the resurrection) spiritual body (15:42-53). The former is perishable; the latter imperishable. The former dies in dishonor but comes back to life in glory. We die to this world in weakness, with limitations and inability to protect ourselves from all the dangers that surround us. We will be reborn in power. Our physical body is from earth, composed of elements that can be analyzed in the chemistry laboratory. The new body will be from heaven and will bear the image of the man of heaven (15:49). Our physical bodies are not meant to be immortal. They are built to last up to 100 years or so at the most. But the spiritual body is immortal, made to last forever. Eternal life is not possible for the bodies in which we presently live. What is perishable and mortal must give way to what is imperishable and immortal (15:53-54). The old body must die like a seed in the ground before the new body can emerge. When that happens death will indeed be swallowed up in victory and will have lost its sting forever (15:54-56).

Paul makes a valiant effort to explain the inexplicable. It is all too wonderful for us. We find comfort in his words, though we still are not clear what all of it means. This much we can say with Paul. Christ has risen from the dead. Those who die in the Lord will also rise to a new life, different from this one but continuous with it. It will be wonderful. God will be there. All enemies, including death, will be swallowed up in victory. Our fear of death can end now as we await the final sound of the trumpet.

## G. Speaking of Hope to Others

"Blessed be the God and Father of our Lord Jesus Christ, the Father of mercies and the God of all consolation, who consoles us in all our affliction, so that we may be able to console those who are in any affliction with the consolation with which we ourselves are consoled by God" (1 Cor. 1:3-4).

God has called us to be comforters one of another. When we see hopelessness in our friends, loved ones, fellow believers, we want to do something to help them renew their hope. What can we say that can make a difference? Are there any words powerful enough, persuasive enough to change another's mind and outlook from despair to hope? Beyond words, what can we do to provide a sign, a symbol or an example, that there is good reason to hope, that the present suffering will pass, that God is still in charge and God is good?

### 1. Listen before speaking (Job 2:11-13)

Too often we are quick to provide answers before we have even heard the questions. We want to move quickly to say something so profound, so beautiful, so irresistable, that despair will melt away to be replaced by the glow of hope. Oh, if only we had that kind of power! It is hard to sit quietly and listen to terrible stories of human torment without trying to barge ahead and fix it, even though we don't really know how to do that. Maybe we will get lucky and say the right thing that will suddenly move our listener back to hope. More often, hope returns slowly over a period of time, not through some sudden miraculous turn around brought on by the inspirational words of the spiritual comforter.

Job's friends heard about his series of calamities and came to offer their comfort. At first, they were so moved by the way he looked that they could only weep in silence with him (Job 2:12-13). Later, after Job bitterly cursed the day that he was born (chapter 3), they couldn't hold back the urge to talk him out of his depression. And so they began to fill the air with words. They pretended to know more than they did. They had been of help to Job when they had enough wisdom to keep silence. When they opened their mouths to speak they moved onto thin ice, offending Job rather than comforting him. Later Job said to them, "If you would only keep silent, that would be your wisdom" (Job 13:5).

A few words about the value of silence for helping to renew hope in another:

(a) We don't have to be professional counselors in order to help others if we simply learn the gift of listening. We may think we are inadequate to the task. We know that we have no great words of wisdom that can change their desperate situation. So we are tempted to stay away from them and not offer the one thing that we can give—our caring presence, a listening ear.

(b) Much can be conveyed between persons without the use of words. People often feel more hopeful after someone has made a commitment to listen to them, to hear them out, to let them tell their story. It may be that no specific word of comfort was spoken and the situation that had led to a feeling of hopelessness has not been resolved. But someone has listened. Hope comes through community, human beings supporting one another and being present with them in times of trouble. We need to have more confidence in the power of presence, of quiet listening, so that we can quelch our impulse to say too much too soon.

(c) Sometimes words spoken by a too eager counselor are not only diverting, tangential, irrelevant. They can even be harmful. This was certainly true in the case of Job. His friends concluded that his pitiful condition was a consequence of his own sinful behavior. Job understood this as condemnation rather than a helpful explanation of his troubles. It may be that a word that has been comforting and renewing to you (possibly even from the Bible) may have a very different response from someone else. One person's profound word of spiritual insight may sound like a pious platitude (or worse) to someone else.

(d) By listening carefully, we may be able to encourage others to rebuild hope from their own resources, not from the clumsy efforts of a well-meaning counselor. Persons in great need of a renewal of hope must do the hard word for themselves, examining their inner lives and their relationships with God and humanity. No one can do it for them, though we can encourage them to do so.

Strangely, we may be more help to someone searching for hope by our silence than by our words. This is both humbling and enabling. It implies limits to our ability to help. It also means that we can be of considerable help even with our ignorance, inadequacy, and lack of professional expertise.

## 2. Don't promise too much

"Like vinegar on a wound is one who sings songs to a heavy heart" (Prov. 25:20a).

Our temptation is to sing a happy song, promise "that everything will be all right," wear a silly grin. But if we want to increase hope for the long haul, and not just for the easing of a particular moment, honesty and realism is the best policy. We may feel the compulsion to say something hopeful when we don't really think or feel that way at all. We are sometimes so concerned to relieve the immediate anxiety and fear of our friend that we promise things that we cannot deliver, assume outcomes which are doubtful, and perhaps even tell untruths (a "little white lie," we call it).

Some adults are still afraid of doctors and dentists because their mothers told them, a long time ago, that this really won't hurt very much. But it did. Not many years ago, doctors were very reluctant to speak honestly to patients about their negative prognosis, defending their lack of candor with the reasoning that they did not want to destroy the patients' hope. And so the dying person, doctor, and family were all forced to play games with each other instead of dealing with realilty and finding hope even in the face of the difficult situation that they must endure together.

A lifelong Christian cannot get rid of a chronic and progressive disease in spite of hours of fervent prayer by a group of close friends. Now he is dismayed because his friends seem to be blaming his lack of faith for his failure to overcome the illness. Could they be right? He had never thought that way before. Now he is confronted by a faith crisis brought on by the insistence of his friends that they had the power to control God and manipulate the course of his disease.

Hope that is built on less than the truth cannot be sustained over the length of our lives. False hopes may seem to hold up well for a time, and if we are lucky, perhaps for a long time. But the reality is that there is danger out there. Sometimes bad things happen no matter what we have done to ensure that our life would go smoothly. Each new day of life is an adventure with many things out of our control. People do get hurt. And sooner or later they will die. The evening news on TV is a constant reminder of the ongoing suffering and pain of the world.

The frustration and disillusionment of smashed hopes can make it very difficult for the revival of hope. If one had expected too much, was naive about the goodness of other people and overly optimistic about our ability to command God to answer our prayers exactly as presented in each petition, then the disappointment can be a great threat to one's trust (faith). If God has failed me in this crisis, how can I be sure that God will be there for the next one? As we have said early on and many times throughout these reflections, hope and faith are very closely related. As Christians, our task is to rebuild trust (and, therefore, hope) in a God who loves us enough to enter into the real world, not an imaginary one where everything is fine and there is always a happy ending. It is within the world of pain and suffering and dashed hopes that God has won the victory. With that assurance, we live in hope.

We can speak with hope and confidence about God without resorting to false hopes that may seem to ease our fears for the moment, but which could lead to unnecesary crises of faith when our expectations are not met. Have courage to speak the truth. Remain firm in the confidence that God, through Christ, intends to save the real world, sinful and evil though it might be. No matter how bad the reality turns out to be, it is not beyond God's power to redeem it. That is our ultimate hope that nothing can destroy.

### 3. When to speak explicitly about hope?

"But how are they to call on one in whom they have not believed? And how are they to believe in one of whom they have never heard? And how are they to hear without someone to proclaim him?" (Rom. 10:14).

Timing is very important in any situation of counseling. This is surely true of our efforts to bring comfort and renew hope. When is the moment in our conversations with others when they will be most receptive to our clear and direct words about a God who meets them in their anguish and promises them a peace that the world cannot give? How long do we keep silent and let the lament continue?

Some argue that you make your witness immediately, as soon as you can, in clear words of proclamation, and then trust the Holy Spirit to bring belief in the listener. This may be your only chance to speak the gospel promise and you mustn't let it pass by without acting. Not to do so betrays a real loss of nerve.

Others, particularly those who have been influenced by their study of psychology, tell us that we must be careful to look for the opportune time to make pronouncements about our faith in Jesus Christ. In our secular world, many people are turned off as soon as the conversation turns to "God talk." Others may perceive our urging to have hope as glib platitudes, superficially offered too soon, as if we are trying to stifle their pain and suffering by proposing too quick a solution. Or, our urging to be hopeful may sound like an impossible task—of course they would be hopeful if they could. They may think that we have not taken their despair seriously enough if we suppose they can move so rapidly into an attitude of hope after hearing a few words about God's wonderful attributes.

A few thoughts on when, in our efforts to renew hope in others, to be explicit in our proclamation of God's promises:

(a) Most of us will probably err on one side or the other, being either too bold or too cautious to speak of matters of faith. We should be aware of our own tendencies so that we can make judgments about when to speak and when to listen that are based on the appropriateness of the situation and not just what makes us feel most comfortable.

(b) It is important to let the lament run its course. Most of us are uneasy with an extended lament, especially when it involves intensive preoccupation with negative emotions, expressions of hostility, or serious challenges to God's goodness and justice. It is hard to resist the impulse to talk them out of their depression or criticize their outbursts of anger or argue with their mistaken ideas of an absent and unjust God. But hurting people may not be responsive toward any of our overtures about a God in whom they should put their hope until they have had the opportunity fully to express their pain. It we are not willing to hear them out, if we seem to be stifling their protest rather than caring what has happened to them, they will be in no mood to hear or understand our words of hope. "First show me you care by listening to me," they say. "Then maybe I can begin to believe there is still reason to hope."

(c) Try to get out of the way and let God speak. If one wants to argue with God, be willing to let that happen without interfering, without jumping to defend God. Listen carefully to the lament as if you were a referee, encouraging the players to engage with each other without injecting yourself into the game. Listen carefully for openings where a specific word from God (perhaps a carefully chosen Bible verse) may speak directly to what someone has been saying as they tell you about their faith struggle. Share that word, but not in a heavy-handed way as if it is a final solution to the problem. Don't over interpret what it means. Let the Holy Spirit work through your presence and whatever words seem appropriate to renew hope. You cannot do it by yourself. If we try to do too much, we may get in the way of what God is trying to do.

It is a fine line to walk between our responsibility to be messengers of a clear word from God and our tendency to get in the way of the word. Sometimes our religious language and pious sentiments make it more difficult for God to speak directly to the one who is in most need of God's assurance. On the other hand, if we say nothing, the person may never hear the good news. With God's help, it is possible to walk that fine line.

### 4. Dare to show your love and concern (1 John 4:10-12)

We can probably make it more complicated than it is. If our motivation is right and we have good common sense, there is a good chance that we will be of considerable help to those who seek to renew hope. If we approach another out of loving concern and we are able to open up and let them know our love for them, we will have some positive effect on their return to hope.

A few closing comments, drawing together some themes that we have examined earlier:

(a) Hope is elusive, mysterious, hard to grasp and control. We can not force ourselves to hope by a mere act of will. And surely we cannot make it happen in others no matter how hard we try, what approach we use, how clever we are with words, how sincere we are in our efforts. When hope is present it is a gift, an act of grace. To live in hope, as in faith, is a wonderful thing and those who are so blessed should thank God every day.

(b) Human communities of support are very important to all of us, but particularly in times of special need—illness and its aftermath, grief, loss, fear, and suffering of all kinds.

(c) There is a place for intellectual arguments about the meaning of suffering. They satisfy our search for meaning and they help us come to some reasonable explanation why a God who can let such terrible things happen can still be a God whom we can trust with our future. But such efforts of the mind are often not the most useful while one is still mired in suffering, not yet able to see hope. More often than not, hope returns slowly through association with other people who listen and understand and share their own spiritual journeys with us. Often, our first glimmer of renewed hope comes when we realize that someone loves us and cares for us. Later, having found strength within that relationship of love, when we are ready, we can resume the daunting intellectual task of trying to make sense out of what has happened in our lives.

(d) We should not worry over much about saying it right, making a blunder, being unable to answer every question that a despairing person throws at us. "I don't know" or "That doesn't make sense to me either" are honest and appropriate responses to many perplexing situations of life. We may even help the one groping for new hope by admitting that we are together in our community of ignorance. If we must worry about something, perhaps it would be better to wonder if we have provided loving relationships of support for the one who seems without hope. We can actually do something about that, though we cannot pretend to answer satisfactorily all the lamenter's questions.

(e) The church can be a community of love in which God's promises are not only proclaimed but are lived in relationships with other believers. If the word that is read from the Bible, preached from the pulpit, and presented in the ritual and sacraments is consistent with the love shown within that community, then that is a place where hope is alive and well. God's work to renew hope will be accomplished more easily there. May we all be blessed to be participants in such a community of grace!

"In this is love, not that we loved God but that he loved us and sent his Son to be the atoning sacrifice for our sins. Beloved, since God loved us so much, we also ought to love one another. No one has ever seen God; if we love one another, God lives in us, and his love is perfected in us" (1 John 4:10-12).